EVERYTHING YOU EVER WANTED TO KNOW ABOUT

*F*ABRIC *P*AINTING

JILL KENNEDY AND
JANE VARRALL

NORTH
LIGHT
BOOKS

Cincinnati, Ohio

First published 1994

© Jill Kennedy and Jane Varrall 1994

Typeset by Goodfellow & Egan Ltd, Cambridge and printed in Hong Kong

Published by
B.T. Batsford Ltd
4 Fitzhardinge Street
London W1H 0AH

First published in the United States by
North Light Books
F & W Publications, Inc.
1507 Dana Avenue
Cincinnati, Ohio 45207
1-800-289-0963

British Library Cataloguing-in-Publication Data. A catalogue record for this book is available from the British Library.

ISBN 0-89134-611-2

ACKNOWLEDGEMENTS

We would like to thank our husbands, Shaun and David, for their help and patience throughout the preparation of the book. Our thanks also go to our parents, who have given time, help and encouragement on many of the projects, as have our children, Thomas, Alexander, Nicholas, Rebecca and Katherine.

Thanks go to our friends – to Sarah for reading, to Charlotte for quilting, to Joanna for sewing, to Jean-Pierre for the photography and to Mary for the typing. Also to our lovely models, Sarah, Sophie, Chantal, Rebecca, Kathryn and Anna.

We would like to thank the following companies for providing some of the materials used in our samples: Arnold NES, Cornellissen, Daler-Rowney, Dupont, Dylon, Hobbidee, Inscribe, Kemtex, Philip and Tacey, George Weil and Whaleys.

The photographs for the book were taken by:

J.P. Van Den Wayenberg
Fotostudio Jean-Pierre
Mechelsesteenweg 232
3060 Sterrebeek
Belgium

CONTENTS

INTRODUCTION

The exciting range of fabric-decorating materials available today from art and craft shops and through mail order should make it easy to create your designs on all sorts of fabrics for all sorts of purposes. You may, however, as a student of textiles or a leisure artist, find yourself bewildered by the array of pots, tubs, bottles, cans, sticks, pens and crayons on offer. We hope that this book will help you to begin each project with a clear idea of your requirements.

We aim to stretch your imagination and skills by introducing you to a variety of painting techniques, each of which is illustrated by designs specifically prepared for this book. As we have taught the techniques to students, as well as practising them ourselves, we have a good idea of the problems which may arise and offer suggestions to cope with most eventualities.

The main body of the book is devoted to techniques – the various and exciting ways of applying colour to fabric. We have grouped these so that you can find your way about the book easily. Some of the techniques require little in the way of specialized equipment, but others do demand special fabrics, chemicals or dye products. For this reason the back of the book includes useful addresses of stockists to help you find unusual products that you may need for your work.

We have researched many techniques for this book which fabric painters may not have attempted before. These include marbling, sun and fire, foil-printing and methods inspired by interior design such as woodgraining, combing and stencilling. We have not neglected traditional techniques such as tie-dye, transfer- and screen-printing, gutta and wax, although we have aimed to modernize and revitalise these.

The reference section at the back of the book discusses fabrics, paints and dyes, fixing and aftercare, the equipment needed, organizing your workplace and safety.

We have very much enjoyed working on this book and hope that you find it stimulating. Painting on fabric offers wonderful design opportunities at all levels of ability. Come on – express yourselves!

A dramatic wallhanging on rose-coloured silk. The tie-dye technique, quilting and embroidery were all combined on this piece

PAINTING
DIRECT

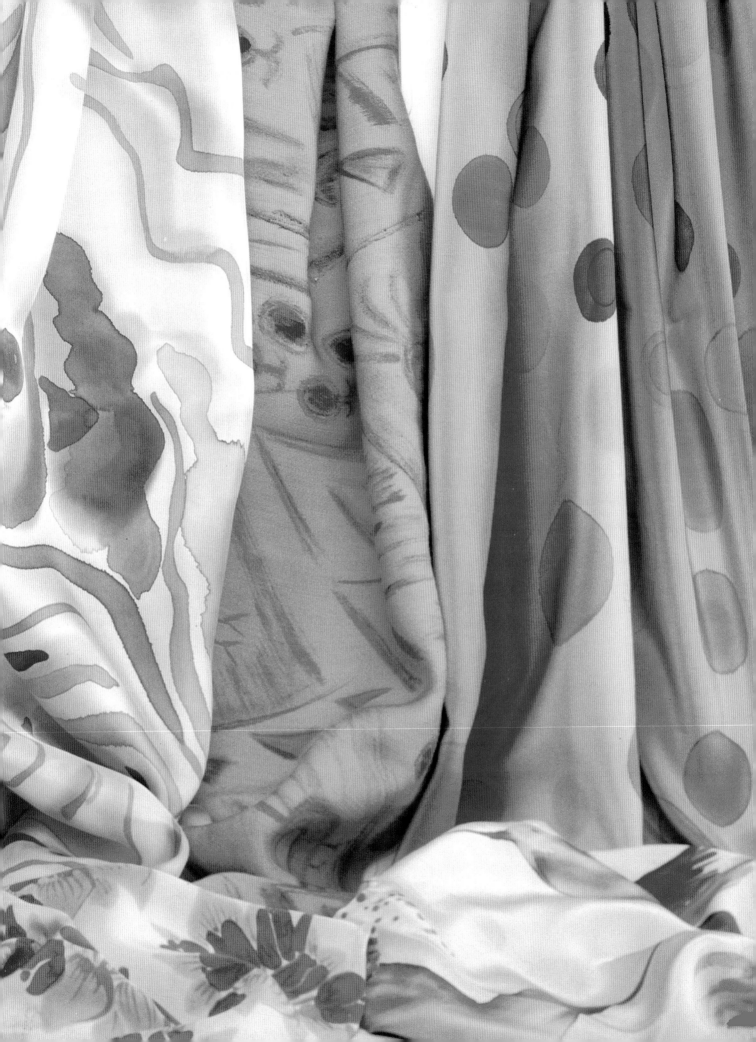

The application of colour to fabric is a very exciting experience. The freedom which this technique gives for playing with colour is amazing; we never cease to be stunned by the depth of hues and shades or the creativity of the textures formed.

Exploring the use of colour on silk, cotton, wool and man-made fabrics has been fascinating. Some of our ideas have been developed from other art forms such as watercolour painting, and have been applied to fabrics with interesting results.

Nothing could be easier than painting directly on to fabric, although prior knowledge of the information given in this book on fabrics, colour and design will improve your results considerably.

Equipment needed

- Fabric
- Water
- Frame, pins, polythene sheeting
- Masking tape
- Dyes and paints
- Diluent, diffusing agent, alcohol and distilled water
- Thickener (épaississant)
- Brushes, applicators, palettes, jars
- Cotton wool
- Hairdryer

Fabrics

The thinner and smoother the fabric, the faster the colours will flow across it. A no. 5 pongée absorbs colour faster than a heavier-weight crêpe de Chine; similarly, a fine lawn absorbs

A landscape painting created with the watercolour technique, and the equipment needed

(*Previous page*)
A collection of fabrics in subtle textures and colours.
(*Top, from left to right*)
    Iron-fixed paints on velvet
    Calico placed on ruched polythene; dyes applied and left to merge and then dry before uncovering
    Steam-fixed silk-painting dyes on twill-weave silk, painted over a wet-on-wet background
    Painting-direct dry-brush technique on yellow/green polyester
    Wet-on-dry dots on a beautifully shaded background
(*Bottom, from left to right*)
    Subtle wet-on-wet tulips
    Delicate over-painted wet-on-dry bunches of tulips
    Carefully shaded birds of paradise on crêpe de Chine

colour faster than a calico. When painting large areas, over-estimate the quantity of dye to be mixed (remembering that the thicker the fabric, the more dye is needed), as matching colours is sometimes impossible.

Dyes and paints

Dyes react in a different way to paints on fabrics; experiment to find a suitable type for your work. Silk-painting dyes, which can be used on the protein fibres of silk and wool, have a depth that can hardly be matched, and they are simple to use. Whenever possible, we use these dyes for this technique of painting on direct. Paints or Procion dyes are alternatives for cotton and man-made fabrics; the paints tend to stiffen the natural feel of the fabric.

Diluting silk-painting dyes

Several manufacturers recommend diluting their dyes, and this does not diminish their brilliance and colour concentration. Read the instructions before use, or you may waste valuable dye and overload the fibres with too much colour. This will run, after fixing, during the washing stage and will ruin your work.

Instead of using water alone to wet the fabric and help the dyes spread evenly, you can buy special liquid called *diluent* (also known as diffusant, fond-net, anticerne, diluant and dilutant). Diluent aids the uniform spreading and merging of the dyes, avoiding hard lines and watermarks. Some silk painters prepare a large bottle of diluent and use it all the time for mixing with the dyes and wetting silk.

An alternative to diluent is the use of alcohol and distilled water. The alcohol may be found under the names of Isopropyl rubbing alcohol or Methanol. The ratio of water to alcohol can vary, but a 50/50 mixture is the most usual.

We have found that the addition of diluent to the dyes keeps the fabric wet for longer than the alcohol mix. Both of them help the blending and even coloration of the fabric tremendously. An advantage of diluent is that it is non-toxic, odourless and non-flammable.

Diluting paints

No advantage has been found by adding diluent or alcohol. The manufacturers suggest simply mixing with water.

Use silk-painting dyes and paints for the following painting-direct techniques. For the purposes of this section, when 'dye' is written, read 'dye and paint'.

FLAT WASH

Mix your colour with diluent to the required hue. It is essential to mix plenty in your palette or jam jar, as the application of the wash needs to be continuous. Stretch the fabric on to a frame, and use either a large brush, a foam applicator, a sponge or cotton wool held in a clothes' peg to apply the colour. A pale colour may necessitate wetting the background with water, or preferably with water and diluent. This allows the brushstrokes to merge into the fabric, avoiding hard edges. Remember that, with a wet background, the hue applied will dry lighter.

At this stage you may find that your fabric has stretched, with the water relaxing the weave. Re-pin so that it is taut on the frame before you start painting. The fabric should not be over-wet, or puddles of dye will collect in the middle, causing back-runs. If it is over-wet, use a ball of cotton wool to wipe over the surface, and wait until the fabric has dried a little but is still damp to the touch before painting.

Paint across the fabric quickly and evenly from side to side, working down the fabric. Overlap your strokes slightly all the way down. When the brush needs re-filling, always re-join at the edge of the fabric, never in the middle, to avoid the build-up of dye in one place.

On thicker fabrics you may need to put more pressure on the brush to 'work' the dye into the fabric. Fabric with a crimp such as crêpe or georgette needs rubbing – do not be afraid to do this. Wool fabric may felt if rubbed excessively.

GRADED WASH

Simple but very effective, a graded wash colours the fabric from dark to light or light to dark. Prepare your hues with diluent and water; between three and five hues will be sufficient. Start with either the lightest or darkest hue. Apply as for the flat wash, achieving a smooth transition from one hue to another. Rub your semi-dry brush over the joins of hue as you progress down the fabric. Never re-rub an area which has dried or back-runs will appear.

GRADING MORE THAN ONE COLOUR

Work as for the graded wash. Paint with one brush, starting with the lightest hue and working down to the darkest. Be careful not to spoil your dye colours by contamination; use several brushes if you prefer.

Two colours can be painted at either end of the fabric and graded to meet softly in the middle.

Samples using the painting-direct technique.
(*Left, from top to bottom*)
   Wet-on-dry (silk)
   Foam brushstrokes (wool)
   Wet-on-dry, building up colours
   with thickened dyes (georgette)
(*Centre, from top to bottom*)
   Tartan wet-on-dry (wool)
   Wet-on-dry wiggles (silk)
   Paints trickled on to fabric; this was
   crumpled and allowed to dry (calico)
   Brushstrokes using thickened heat-
   fixed dyes (wild silk)
(*Right, from top to bottom*)
   Fabric laid on polythene and
   crumpled; dye applied and allowed
   to dry (furnishing repp)
   Over-painting using thickened
   paints (georgette)
   Wet-on-wet (silk)

MOTTLED OR VARIEGATED WASH

A mottled wash makes a very useful background texture. As it dries, certain pigments separate out and mix with other hues in an interesting way. We have noticed that traces of red are seen when using brown or green dyes.

This technique is especially effective when painting skies. Wet the fabric and roll a dye-filled brush over the surface in different directions. Add plenty of diluent or water as you work, and use a variety of colours to accentuate the clouds. The fabric can be left to dry naturally, but if an atmospheric effect has been achieved already, dry the fabric immediately or the clouds may continue to blend during the drying process and will be lost.

A sponge can give some unpredictable results when used to apply the dyes if you vary the concentration of colour.

Charming underwear ideas in crêpe de Chine

WET-ON-WET

This is a very simple technique which produces a soft but lively effect. Experience will tell you how wet the background should be; more control is gained when the background is drier. When used in combined techniques, for example with wax or particularly antifusant, the soft effect will be sharpened.

Dampen the fabric with diluent, a colour or a graded wash. While this background is still wet, apply one or more colours to create a pattern or design. Apply fairly strong colours: over-diluted colours tend to look rather washed out, while rich colours look most effective. The dyes vary in their speed of spreading.

Water and flowers adapt well to this technique, giving an impressionistic interpretation to your work. As long as the fabric remains wet, a fluid, diffused look results. The merging of just a few colours creates unexpected hues, tints, tones and shades. Place lines of colour side by side, and allow them to blend and merge. Drop blobs of colour over the wet surface and let them mingle. Leave white areas and let colour trickle down on to them.

WET-ON-DRY (over-painting, overlaying, glazing)

This is the technique of painting one colour over another colour that is dry. It can also be used after painting a wet-on-wet background to create sharp, definite forms.

Paint a pale background colour or colours. Dry this, and then apply several strengthening tones of colour. By painting a colour and drying between each application, an idea of perspective can be built up on the fabric, which is very useful for creating depth and space in monochromatic landscapes.

As each darker layer is painted and dried, you will notice that the dye is pushed to the drying edge, sometimes forming a feathery or hard, jagged outline. These lines create a texture and are worth saving by drying the piece quickly with a hairdryer. This technique is sometimes known as *line building*. When water or diluent is applied on top of a dry, painted wash, whether by re-painting, flicking, dripping or puddling, lines are also created; these are known as *back-runs*.

Stripes and tartans build up easily using wet-on-dry techniques. The background, when coloured, unifies the whole fabric, but remember that the underlying colour will affect the colours painted on top. These will need to be stronger,

as some may neutralize each other and produce rather muddy tones.

A lovely effect is created when using transparent silk-painting dyes, especially on shiny silks such as satin, twill or pongée. Being transparent, the colours reflect through each other. Start with a pale colour. When it is absolutely dry, overlap a second colour. Where the colours cross each other, a third is formed. This is known as *glazing*. The effect can be continued using the anti-spread technique (see page 47).

SHADING, DOUBLE-LOADING AND DRY-BRUSHING

These techniques are important when used in conjunction with the gutta technique (see pages 41–7). The dyes are restricted, so the shading within the shapes created can be subtle. Remember that a little dye goes a long way; never overload your brush as you will flood the area, giving no opportunity for varying the shade or colour. A fine-pointed Chinese brush is essential.

There are several ways of shading your work. First select your colours (small quantities of dye in a palette are usually sufficient). When painting a flower, for example, select one main hue and lighter and darker

shades of that hue. Also choose a little of two other hues which could highlight the flower. Paint your flower either from dry or from wet. We usually paint from dry, but many painters produce very subtle shading when painting on a surface which has been wetted by diluent or alcohol. Remember that colour on a wet background will dry much lighter.

Start to shade the flower by painting over any areas you wish to remain pale or white with diluent to stop the dye from flowing into them. Place some of the strong colour on the tip of your brush and blend it down towards the diluent. Rinse away the strong hue and dry your brush quickly on some absorbent tissue. Take a little of the medium tone and continue shading towards the diluent; do the same with the tint. Finally, dry your brush and continue to blend the colours lightly together. While these are wet, touches of the other hues can be added. Alcohol on a cotton bud can remove excess dye where you may have been heavy-handed.

Producing the shading is the most exciting part of fabric painting. An interesting method is to put two or even three colours on to your brush at the same time, which is sometimes called *double-loading*. Place your brush into a dye colour, then point the tip into a second. When you place the tip of the brush on to the fabric, press downwards, increasing the

pressure and width of the brushstroke. The second colour will merge and blend with the first to create new colours. A large leaf or petal shape can come to life using this technique.

Another idea to vary your shading is to put thickened dye on to the ready-painted shape. The *dry-brush* technique, in which dye is applied sparingly on a dry brush, is very useful for adding extra strength of colour. If it is too wet, you will create lines as in the wet-on-dry

technique. Left-over dyes which are drying in palettes or jars are suitable, as are the thicker iron-fixed dyes. Very fine detailing can be applied using this method.

ÉPAISSISSANT (thickener)

Épaississant is a colourless, glue-like substance, also known as dye thickener. This thickener can be added to dyes, making it

Painting direct on cotton using fabric paints

possible to paint directly on to fabric without the dyes spreading. Pour a small amount of thickener into a palette and mix with the dye as required. This thickened dye is useful for dry-brush work. Do not use it on large areas, as uneven coloration will result. Textures can be created with this thickened dye (see pages 78 and 91), increasing its use tremendously.

ADDITIVES

We have grouped the techniques in this chapter together under the heading of 'Additives', as all of them are similar in that they require something to be placed on to the painted fabric. The additives: salt (the grains), sun (the masks), fire (the flame), bleach (the liquid) and metallic granules (the powder) all affect the dye or fabric. Very different reactions from each will develop your, perhaps conventional, ideas of what the term fabric painting means. Each one may be used with other techniques, or entirely on its own.

(*Previous page*)
An array of fabrics painted with additives.
(*From left to right and top to bottom*)
 Concentrated bleach on a double-painted blue cotton ground. The top layer is bleached, revealing frosty turquoise undercolours
 Softly painted shades of purple flowers and green leaves on *etamine de laine* (pure wool), strongly outlined with alcohol brushstrokes
 Vivid blue sea-salt-crystal texture on shimmering pongée silk
 Nylon net delicately painted in pastel blues, highlighted on the clouds by metallic powder
 Sunlight technique reflecting the luxurious purple-grey colour of the satin; stately figures and beads have resisted the sun
 Dramatic slashes of flame-like holes cut an extra dimension in this brightly painted polyester

SALT-CRYSTAL AND SALT-SOLUTION EFFECTS

Equipment needed

- Fabric
- Salt
- Water
- Frame and pins
- Masking tape
- Dyes and paints
- Brushes, droppers, palette, jars
- Cotton wool
- Hairdryer

(*Above*)
Some of the equipment needed, with fabric samples.
(*Left*)
 Spirals and swirls made with a foam brush on an impregnated-salt background
(*Centre*)
 Top: bright sea-salt wheel
 Middle: pastel brushstrokes with bleach on fine cotton
 Bottom: bold green leaves on silk created using the sun technique
(*Right*)
 Thousands of alcohol drops on rich purples and greens

Dyes and paints

Salts work well on deeper colours at the recommended maximum concentration of the dye or paint, producing strong lines and shapes. Pale colours such as pink and grey do not react well on their own and will need to merge with stronger dyes to be effective. Do not dilute the colours too much with diluent. Alcohol should not be used, as the salt needs time to work and alcohol dries too fast.

We have found that some colours react much better than others. Dark dye colours, such as brown, green, navy and maroon, really move well, whereas yellow and purple do not. The separating out of the colour pigment creates a good effect; with brown, for instance, this produces pinky-red edges. Black very rarely works, and it is risky to apply it heavily to try to create an effect as it may not be absorbed into the fabric and could wash out after fixing.

SALT CRYSTALS

Dramatic salt-crystal effects are the most exciting when used on silk fabrics, but we have had some good results on wool and, to a lesser extent, on cotton. It is probably the easiest of all techniques. Simply paint the fabric; the salt attracts the moisture and pulls the dye or paint in various directions, creating marvellous textures. The end result is often beyond your control, but there are a few hints which can help you to place the effects where you most want them.

Table salt produces a fine, feathery effect and is valuable for creating texture within gutta-resist shapes such as leaves and petals. Coarse sea salt is the ideal choice for more dramatic effects. Pearl-salt grains, being uniform in size, produce a more even, rounded design. Special salt for use with this technique can also be bought from silk-painting manufacturers; this salt works well with iron-fixed paints.

Salt techniques.
(*From left to right*)
Striped bands of sea salt
Randomly painted background and sea salt
Crêpe de Chine flowers
Flowers and leaves created with table and sea salt
Geometric shapes on a salt-impregnated background

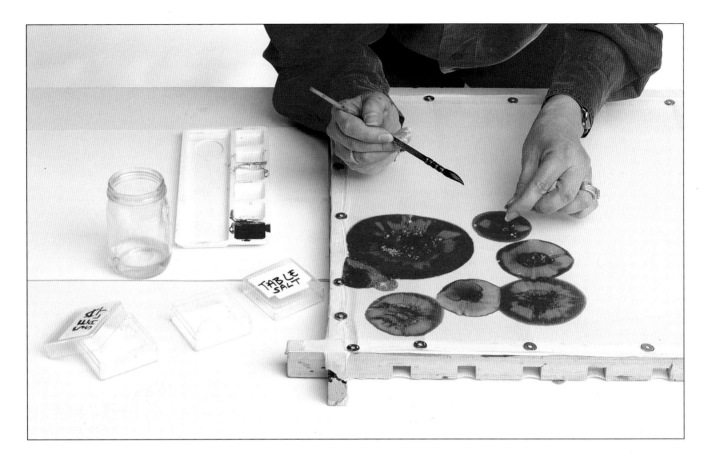

Salt reacting to dye. Circles are painted and then immediately sprinkled with salt

The coarse salt can be dried and re-used, but it will be discoloured. Never allow dye which has been contaminated by salt to be poured back into its original bottle, as the dye will not flow smoothly on to fabric. It can be used for other salted backgrounds.

Applying the salt

Stretch the fabric on to a frame and paint the fabric with your colours. It is important to wet the fabric, but do not saturate it.

Quickly sprinkle the salt over the surface of the damp fabric, using your fingers with coarse salt or a shaker for fine salt. Be careful not to use too much salt, as this will hinder the reaction and it will be indistinct; likewise, too little salt will not create enough texture.

Always use the salt technique last on combined pieces of work. It is frustrating if a grain appears on an area which you wanted to be plain, such as the border of a scarf.

Salt reactions

Stripes

Paint stripes with a foam applicator or a brush, and place

rock, sea or table salt along the joins. Do not wait until all the lines are painted – add salt as you go along.

Circles or flowers

Paint the background and, while wet, place accurate circles of salt on the surface. Drop or paint another colour in the middle. Alternatively, place the salt on dry fabric and add the colour afterwards – this method is trickier, but lovely flower shapes are formed. The salt can also be applied to the centre of two-coloured circles.

Leave the fabric undisturbed (this may take up to half an hour). Salting fabric outdoors is not recommended, as the sun may dry it too fast and the breeze may disturb the salt.

Hints for controlling the results

The effect will be different depending on:

- the colour chosen
- the brand of dye or paint
- the wetness/dryness of colour on the fabric
- the type and thickness of fabric
- the tautness of the fabric on the frame
- the size of salt
- the amount of salt
- the room temperature and humidity

While watching your fabric dry, you may wish to stop the salt from reacting further. If so, tip the frame over quickly and tap off the salt from the back on to the table. Dry the fabric with a hairdryer to prevent further movement.

When the fabric is completely dry, remove all the salt from the surface by brushing it away. When fixing with a steamer (see pages 121–2), use a double sheet of paper in order to absorb the moisture from the salt.

SALT SOLUTION

Less dramatic than the salt-crystal technique but with distinct qualities of its own, salt solution is easy to use.

To make the solution, stir 250 g (9 oz) of table salt into one litre (1¾ pints) of lukewarm water.

Stir and leave it to dissolve. Either soak the fabric in this solution and then hang it up to dry, or stretch the fabric on to a frame and paint the solution on to it using a large brush, sponge or cotton wool. Leave it to dry. When dry, the fabric sparkles with tiny dots of salt crystals.

Beautiful, luxurious over-blouses. The left-hand blouse is printed in deep blue on crêpe de Chine with a sea-salt texture at the hemline. The right-hand blouse is in a graded grey wash, more heavily sea-salted, on heavyweight pongée

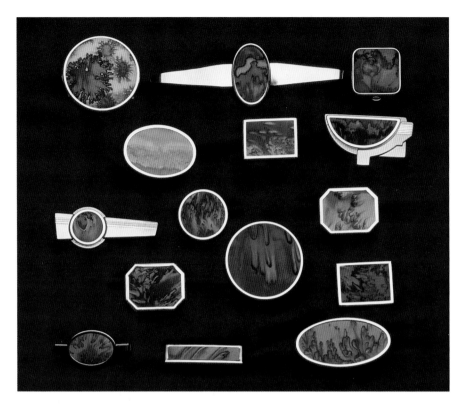

A wonderful collection of brooches, boxes, bracelets and buckles highlighting the exciting results of the salt technique. Each one is an original, as no two examples can be the same

When painting the salt-impregnated background, take care to apply only tiny dots of colour. If the brush is over-loaded with dye the salt effect will disappear. A foam brush used quickly will give more geometric shapes. The salt restricts the flow of the colours.

Try experimenting by painting the fabric while the solution is still damp. The dye dries with a small scallop or zig-zag, and small, dainty white spots can be seen.

SUN

Light-reactive dyes work extremely effectively on cotton and silk. Only one or two brands of paints work with this technique, so you will need to test them before embarking on a specific project.

Equipment needed

- Fabric
- Water
- Setacolour transparent dyes
- Found and natural objects
- Templates
- Light source: sun, halogen lamp, sun lamp or infra-red lamp
- Brushes
- Paper or card
- Scissors

Sun technique

This pretty technique should really be saved for the summer, but sunlight can be replaced by an alternative light source indoors, such as strong lamps.

Stretch your fabric on to a frame and dampen the surface with water (there is no need to add diluent for this technique). Dilute the dyes with water: one volume of dye and up to two volumes of water, depending on the strength of colour you require. Quickly paint the entire surface of your fabric with blended or mottled washes of colour, then place on to the wet fabric a template or object which will resist the sunlight. Place the frame in strong sunshine or under lamps to dry. Do not disturb your objects until the fabric is completely dry.

When it is dry, remove the objects. The light will have reacted with the dye, with the areas of fabric under the templates or objects being light in colour and their outer edges sharply defined against the stronger background colour.

Resists for sunlight

Natural forms

- Waxy leaves from houseplants, ferns and conifer branches
- Feathers, large and small – peacock feathers are particularly effective
- Flowers and petals
- Pasta: shells, bows, hoops and spaghetti

Man-made objects
- Grills, grids or lattice-work
- Lace, net, scrim or distorted hessian
- Scissors, buttons, bottles, lids, curtain rings and beads

Home-made templates
- Card and pinking shears
- Overlapped rectangular or geometric shapes
- Simple flower shapes: roses, tulips and daisies
- Stencils

Fabrics which have a sheen are particularly effective with the subtle light-reactive dyes. Fix the dyes with a hot iron.

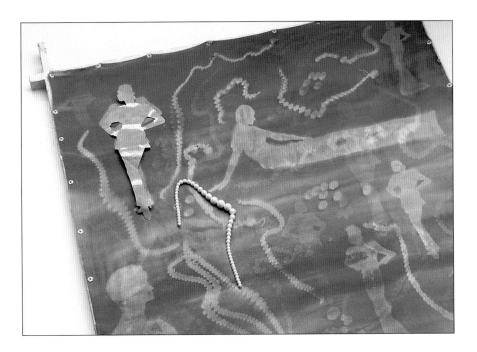

- Cotton wool
- Hairdryer
- Fire blanket

Detail of a piece painted using the sun technique, showing the positioning of a hand-cut template and draped beading

FIRE
(burning and branding)

Although not strictly a 'painting' technique, fire does produce colour by burning shades into the fabric. These effects can be incorporated with your dyes, paints and crayons.

Equipment needed

- Fabric
- Fire: matches, hot plate
- Branding equipment: wire, metal shapes, poker
- Iron
- Frame and pins
- Masking tape
- Dyes, paints, crayons
- Water
- Brushes, droppers, palettes, jars

Applying the fire

Great care is obviously needed with this technique, as working with unguarded flames on fabric is always a danger. Have water or extinguishing equipment available in case an emergency should arise. The following suggestions will all create exciting effects.

- The burning of fabric will create yellow/brown/black textural effects. With a naked match flame, try singeing the edges of calico or canvas to create an antique look.

- Heat up metallic shapes such as nails or bolts and place them on fabric, stamping designs on to the surface in regular or free patterns.

- Twist up wire into your own shapes, heat it and print on to the fabric.

- Colour the fabric with dyes, paints or crayons before or after burning. Remember that some paints, when burned, will flare up and create toxic fumes. If you are unsure, apply your colours after burning.

- Burning and branding on man-made fabric will cause it to shrivel up and disintegrate. Cotton, linen and wool would be worth experimenting with.

- Place painted fabrics behind holes to create three-dimensional effects. Use transparent fabrics for a soft, layered look.

ALCOHOL

Creating dimension in your painting is important, and the more you paint, the more you will master the shading techniques. Alcohol is another medium which can help you to acquire texture and depth of shading. As with salt, you can use a little alcohol to highlight specific areas, or it can be used over an entire piece of fabric.

The effect of alcohol is similar to that of the watercolour technique: the steam-fixed dyes are pushed away by the alcohol when it is applied to the surface. The dyes react more strongly with alcohol than with water. The colour lightens and the centre becomes clear, with the dye pigments building up at the edges and appearing much darker. If this process is repeated several times, the centre becomes increasingly lighter and the outer line more defined.

Equipment needed

- Fabric
- Alcohol: Methanol, Ethyl rubbing alcohol (70%), Isopropyl alcohol, methylated spirit, medicinal alcohol, surgical spirit
- Water
- Dyes: silk-painting transparent

Amber, purple and green waves of colour, textured with alcohol dots, on a permanently pleated crêpe-de-Chine skirt and throw-over scarf

- Frame and pins
- Masking tape
- Diluent
- Brushes, applicators, palettes, jars
- Eco-spray or mouth diffuser
- Cotton wool
- Hairdryer

Fabrics

Silk or wool can be used. Wild silk, with its slub weave, will produce irregular results, so dots and circles will be difficult to obtain. A pre-patterned silk such as jacquard weave would not show this effect to advantage, as the patterning in the fabric would counteract the texture created by the alcohol. We love using this technique on crêpe de Chine for the most rewarding results.

Dyes

This technique only works with steam-fixed silk-painting dyes. We have had no good results with other types of paint. The dyes need to be applied before the fabric is fixed so that they can move. Alcohol reacts better on strong, deep colours, but will give delicate effects on the more pastel tints.

Types of alcohol

The alcohol used in our samples is Methanol (this is obtainable in Europe in DIY shops). Alternatives are Ethyl rubbing alcohol (70%) or Isopropyl alcohol (obtainable in the USA); these may need a permit in some countries. If pure alcohol is obtained it can be diluted with water. The weaker the solution, the poorer the reaction. Alternatives such as methylated spirit, medicinal alcohol and surgical spirit can be used, and should be available at chemists.

Remember that all these products are inflammable; they should be stored and used with the greatest of care. We do not recommend the over-use of alcohol on fabric, as soaking could result in deterioration of the fibres.

Creating alcohol dots with a foam spatula

Brushes and applicators

Experiment with ways of applying alcohol to the silk or wool. We have used all types of brushes, from fine to thick and stiff, fan-shaped brushes. Cotton wool or cotton buds are ideal for dots, and a fine spattering effect can be created with an Eco-spray or mouth diffuser. Foam brushes and sponges are also useful.

Applying the alcohol

Stretch the silk or wool on to a frame and paint with dye. Make sure that the fabric is bone-dry before putting on the alcohol, or a crisp shape will not appear.

Paint on the alcohol with a brush or foam applicator. Tap off the excess on a tissue, and then gently rub the surface of the fabric. The alcohol spreads further on some colours and fabrics than others, so it is wise to test the spread before you start. If the reaction is not sufficient, dry the fabric and re-apply the alcohol. This will bleach out the dye further and create a stronger halo.

Have fun building up circular patterns with a cotton bud, or stripes with a foam applicator. Create texture to camouflage unevenly painted backgrounds, or highlight petals and leaf veins. Dribble alcohol from a brush or pipette for random lines, and repeat again and

Alcohol sample sheet.
(*Left, from top to bottom*)
    Bold plantain leaves on a pink crêpe background. The veining was added with a brush
    Alcohol dots made with a foam spatula
    Horizontal, vertical and then diagonal bands created with a foam brush
    Random trails on slubbed silk
(*Centre, from top to bottom*)
    Random dripping
    Circles on wool
    Dots-on-dots on a jewel-coloured background
(*Right, from top to bottom*)
    Tartan-effect green and blue stripes on wool, made with a foam brush
    Crashing waves on wool, painted with a brush
    Stripes on slubbed silk
    Alcohol squirted through a pipette on to wool

again to push the dyes into crusty ridges. Overlap layer on layer of straight bands using a foam brush for a more geometric style. Stipple the surface with sponges and absorbent paper, or dry-brush areas. These techniques can all be tried using water as an alternative to alcohol (water will be more successful than alcohol on fabric paints).

BLEACH (discharge-dyeing)

With this technique, colour is removed from previously dyed fabric to create textures and patterns. The colour could be painted previously by yourself or could be bought fabric. Household bleach is widely available. The degree of discharge will vary depending on the strength of the bleach.

Equipment needed

- Fabric: coloured, pre-painted or discharge fabrics
- Discharging agents: bleach, Dygon, discharging paste, colour remover (thiourea dioxide)
- Dyes
- Rubber gloves, apron, goggles, face-mask
- Newspaper, plastic sheeting
- Pipettes, brushes, stamps, stencils
- Water
- Thickener: Manutex

Fabrics

Procion dyes (fibre-reactive dyes) only work on natural fibres, so cotton, wool and linen could be used. Silk will take these dyes, but is destroyed by bleach.

Manufacturers have produced a specially treated fabric called prima broadcloth, normally sold in black and navy. It is available by mail order from specialists (see page 127).

Experiment with different strengths of bleach on these fabrics to vary the depth of colour removed; lovely brown to cream shades will appear.

Applying bleach to specially treated black fabric

Discharging agents

WARNING: *all chemicals are dangerous. Keep them away from children and pets.*

Assemble your equipment. Wear rubber gloves, an apron and a face-mask. If there is a danger of bleach splashing in your eyes, wear goggles as well. Cover the floor and your worksurfaces with plastic sheeting or newspaper.

Experimentation is the key to this technique, as it is difficult to predict which dyes will discharge. Most industrial dyes will do so, as will fibre-reactive dyes (Procion) and direct dyes. You must test the fabric and the dyes you wish to use to check their effectiveness. Some dyes will lighten sufficiently for over-dyeing, but will not remove altogether.

Bleach
Dilute the bleach to half-strength if bought in a concentrated form. Eau de Javel (bleach) which is sold on the Continent is not as concentrated as good-quality British bleach, and will therefore not need to be diluted as much.

Thicken bleach with a binder for printing or stamping designs on to fabric. Neutralize the bleach when dry by rinsing the fabric in a weak solution of metabisulphate.

Discharge paste
This is a thick paste which is printed or brushed on to the fabric. It will lighten or change the colour of fibre-reactive dyes. When dry, iron the fabric, then

Bleach sample sheet.
(*Left, from top to bottom*)
   Under-colours exposed with bleach
   Rag-rolling with bleach solution
   Dygon applied with a paintbrush
(*Centre, from top to bottom*)
   Painting on bleach
   A stiff brush used with bleach
   Sponge shapes soaked in bleach
   Frost formation created with full-strength bleach
(*Right, middle and bottom*)
   Wax substitute squeezed through the nozzle of a plastic bottle
   Splashing with medium-strength bleach

wash out any excess to reduce the stiffness. The effects are striking.

Colour remover

Colour can be removed from most cotton, rayon, linen and blends which have been dyed by fibre-reactive dyes. Some dyes will only lighten. Colour remover also strips colour from yarn.

Place 15 ml (one tablespoon) of soda ash (fixer) and 2·5 ml (half a teaspoon) of soft washing-up liquid into three litres (5¼ pints) of water. Add the fabric and bring to the boil. Simmer and add 1·25 ml (quarter of a teaspoon) of colour remover every fifteen minutes for an hour. The colour will gradually be removed.

Alternatively, use a product such as Dygon mixed with a quarter quantity of water, heat it and brush on to the fabric.

Applying the discharging agent

We have already mentioned the use of brushes, but any number of utensils can be used to create texture, from foam cut-out pads to crumpled fabric or chamois leather. Rollers, sticks, feathers,

metal objects – all could be coated with or dipped into bleach. Spray diffusers, straws and pipettes can spatter bleach over a fabric surface.

METALLIC POWDERS

We have used metallic paints and glitter paints extensively later on in the book, but there are also powders available which can highlight your work and create some lovely effects.

The major disadvantage is that the powders rub off unless combined with another medium. Items which are framed, behind glass, will create no problem, but tactile objects or wearable art need the addition of a binder. A bronze binder is available from specialist shops (see pages 126–7). When dry, the binder changes from a rather sludgy opaque glue to a transparent hard surface through which the metallic colours shine.

Application of powders

Use any printing method such as rollers, blocks, card or even vegetables. Paint on the

powders using brushes, or dab the fabric surface with sponges covered in powder. Refer to pages 79–82 for further ideas.

CYANOTYPE (blue-printing, sun-printing)

This fascinating method of printing was invented by Sir John Heschel in 1840 for producing architectural and mechanical drawings. The beautiful shades of blue which are created distinguish it from any other technique. The chemicals which are applied to the fabric (or paper) give it the wonderful hue when exposed to sunlight. An unusual process, this method is often used by quiltmakers, but has been developed into an art form by embroiderers and artists in recent years.

Pre-treated fabrics are now available which make the image-making side easier and quicker for the fabric painter. The chemicals are available in kit form too (see page 127). Your results will be unique and will trap images from the past for ever.

RESISTS

Depending on the various types and how thickly they are applied, resists will prevent the dyeing of the areas of fabric over which they are applied. Any product which adheres to the fabric and prevents the dye from spreading could work as a resist. In this chapter we discuss several methods of resist, all differing in their ability to 'stop' the dye. Wax, string, gutta, sugar, flour, wax substitutes and even masking fluid can be used to prevent the dyes and paints from reaching the areas of fabric that you do not wish to colour.

WAX

The most widely known technique of using hot wax and dyes is batik. This involves waxing the fabric and then immersing the cloth in a dyebath. This process can be repeated several times, with each additional colour being dyed over the previous one.

There are various other techniques involving the use of wax: splattering, scratching, controlled cracking and false batik, in which dyes are painted directly on to the fabric instead of dipping the fabric into a dyebath.

Equipment needed

- Fabric
- Dyes
- Wax
- Wax heater
- Tjanting/tjap applicators
- Iron and paper
- Frame and pins

Fabrics

Natural fabrics work well, especially if you are using the dyebath-immersion method. Use lightweight cotton, silk or calico. Before dyeing, it is best to stretch the fabric on a frame or lay it on greaseproof paper so that the wax does not pass through on to your table.

Dyes

Fabric dyes requiring cold and warm water can be used for this technique, but not the ones which need very hot water. Special batik dyes are also available. Procion dyes produce excellent results and can be used for immersing the fabric or for

---

Equipment for resist techniques.
(*From left to right*)
  Wax
  Sugar
  Tie-dye
  Gutta

(*Previous page*)
Painted fabric using different resists.
(*Clockwise from top left*)
  Wax dolphins on a turquoise background
  Tie-dye: hand-gathered and sprayed
  Gutta technique outlining bright penguins
  Paste-resist stylized circles
  Resist used to create decorative shells
  Sugar stripes in blue
  Masking fluid on heavy satin fabric

painting on to the fabric (see pages 116–18 for the methods of mixing the dyes for both of these procedures). Different manufacturers have their own recipes for their brand of dye. Silk-painting dyes and watered-down fabric paints can also be used in the painting-on method.

Types of wax

Batik wax is a mixture of paraffin wax and beeswax. Paraffin wax is white in colour and can be bought as candles, blocks, powder or beads. It can be found in hardware shops, craft shops or candlemakers' suppliers. Beeswax is more expensive and is yellow in colour.

Preparation of wax

Paraffin wax can be used alone, but when it dries on fabric it is very brittle and has a tendency to peel off. The addition of beeswax to paraffin wax makes a more malleable blend that does not peel off.

Mix six parts paraffin wax to four parts beeswax for a good mix for line work. Depending on the required end result, these quantities can be varied. Heavier crackle will be achieved by increasing the ratio of paraffin wax. A smooth, plain area can be obtained by using beeswax only. A ready-prepared batik wax is also available, and is of course ideal for these techniques.

Heating wax

Wax should not be heated over a naked flame. An electric ring with a double boiler is quite adequate, but the best method is to buy a specially designed wax-melting pot. This can keep the melted wax at a constant temperature of 120°C (248°F).

Painted fabric using wax.
(*From left to right*)
  Tjap
  Spots
  Sgraffito
  Checks
  Slashes
  Tjanting
  Colour words

As the wax is applied to the fabric it should leave a transparent line. If the wax sits on the surface of the fabric, remaining hard and white or cream-coloured, it has not penetrated the fibres of the fabric. If the wax is too hot, it will spread too far and your brushes will quickly be ruined.

Tools and applicators

Brushes, toothbrushes and cotton buds can all be used. Tjantings (cantings) and tjaps (caps) can be bought in specialist craft shops (see pages 126–7) to apply the wax.

(*Opposite page*)
Waxing areas which are to remain yellow with a brush

(*Right*)
Batik fish: stage-by-stage.
(*Top left*)
  The design is drawn on to the fabric
(*Top right*)
  The areas which are to remain white are covered with wax
(*Bottom left*)
  The areas which are to remain yellow are waxed
(*Bottom right*)
  The areas which are to remain orange are waxed

(*Top left*)
  The areas which are to remain red are waxed
(*Top right*)
  The fabric is dyed or painted black
(*Bottom left*)
  The wax is removed by ironing
(*Bottom right*)
  The finished batik fish

TRADITIONAL BATIK

The series of fish designs below aims to show the process of traditional batik. When using hot wax, try to keep it as near to you as possible. Keep a tissue handy to prevent drips of wax from spoiling your work, as the colour under every drip of wax will be preserved.

When choosing the colours for your project, you must plan in advance so that you can apply them in the right order. Start with the lightest colour, and then progress to the darker colours. It is a good idea to make a sample strip to test your dyes as you go, because, when the dyes are overlaid, they mix to create a new colour. For

example, when green is painted over red, a brown is obtained; when blue is painted over yellow, a green is obtained.

It is possible to create contrasting colours on your work, but this will involve dry-cleaning and re-waxing half-way through your project.

FALSE BATIK

For those of you who find traditional batik rather time-consuming and restrictive, it is possible to paint as many colours as you like on to your fabric before waxing, using the paint-on method. You can

repeat the process of applying different colours, waxing to keep them and applying more colours as many times as you wish. This method is sometimes known as false or faux batik, as you can still obtain cracking and a batik-like effect, but without the effort of traditional batik.

TJANTING WORK

The tjanting, or canting, is a small copper bowl attached to a wooden handle with one or more spouts leading from its base. The tool is dipped into hot wax to fill the reservoir and then applied to fabric. Keep a tissue handy to prevent drips of wax from falling from the underside of the bowl. A thin, even, transparent line should be formed. Sometimes the spout blocks as the wax solidifies in the bowl. If this happens, clear the spout with a fine wire or leave the tjanting in the hot wax for a while.

Long, flowing lines or small, intricate designs can be achieved with a tjanting (see the jellyfish and seahorse designs below and opposite). Tjanting work takes practice and mistakes are difficult to remove, but these can sometimes be made to form part of the design.

TJAP WORK

The tjap, or cap, is a copper printing block mounted on wood. It is commonly found in Indonesia and is used for repeat designs. The tjap is not dipped into molten wax, but pressed on to a wax-soaked pad before being placed on the fabric.

You can try making your own metal block by bending wire. You can even print on the wax using a fork or a potato masher.

CRACKING

The characteristic texture created by cracking the wax can enhance your fabric. Depending

Using a tjanting to create colourful jellyfish

A stunning underwater theme on colourful sarongs, created with wax techniques using a tjanting and brush

on the design, you can crack isolated areas or a whole piece of work. To produce the cracking, either just crumple or scrunch the work, or pleat or fold the fabric to obtain a controlled or uniform crackle. The wax must be dry and hard before cracking. Take care on pale, delicate designs, as the dye may penetrate the cracking too thoroughly and ruin the design. Very large, bright backgrounds can be subdued with cracking, however, and hold the design together.

It is possible to achieve several colour crackings by coating each set of crackings with wax and re-cracking and re-dyeing.

SCRATCHING

A design can be etched into a pre-waxed fabric. Coat the entire area with wax and then, using a pointed metal tool (not too sharp or you will rip the fabric), scratch your design into the wax. You can scratch and cross-hatch and produce a detailed linear drawing. Immerse the fabric in a dyebath or paint on the dyes, and the etched line will show up nicely. Remove the wax by ironing, fix if using silk or fabric paints, and dry-clean. This process is also known as *sgraffito*.

WAX SUBSTITUTES

These are used in the same way as wax, the advantage being that they do not need to be heated.

They can be applied with brushes, stamps, sponges or squeezed from a bottle. They can also be used for screen- and block-printing. If the resist is painted thickly over a large area, it wrinkles the fabric. Wax substitutes are rather like the water-based guttas and sugar syrup in that they are diluted with water. A soft, mottled effect can be obtained if they are thinly applied.

A very fine cracking can be achieved by covering the fabric with a layer of resist and, when it is dry, stretching the fabric to form cracks in the resist. Paint over this with dye and you will see very fine lines.

You can steam-fix work coated in wax substitute, although it may stick to the fixing paper. This resist is removed from the fabric by soaking in water and then washing. Remember that these wax substitutes are soluble in water, so you cannot use them in dyebaths.

FLOUR RESISTS

Flour resists are cheap and work well with fabric paints. Fabric and silk dyes are not a good idea because of the steam-fixing needed; the resist sometimes goes rather gooey. You can make these resists yourself by simply mixing flour and cold water to a smooth paste. It tends to disintegrate when drying on the fabric, but you can try adding a drop of glycerine to make it

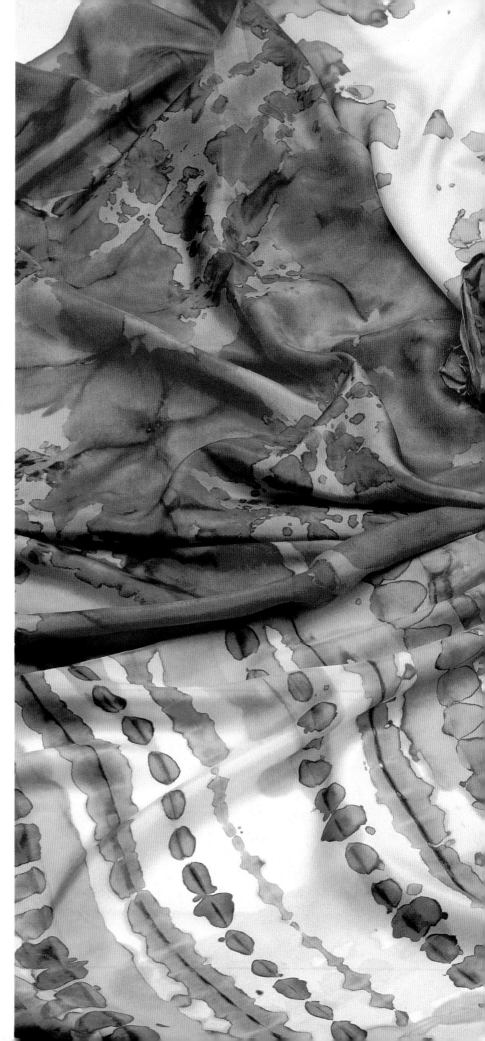

pliable. You can either heat the flour paste or use it uncooked to obtain slightly different results.

After applying the resist to the fabric using a bottle, brush or spreader, paint the fabric, wait until it is dry and then scrape off the excess resist. After fixing, rinse to remove the remains of the flour. Resists can also be made of laundry starch and rice flour.

MASKING FLUID

Masking fluid, which is used to preserve 'clean' areas of paper in watercolour painting, can also be used as a resist on fabric. Small areas only are advisable as, once the dyes have been applied, it is necessary to remove the masking fluid by rubbing it off with your finger or an eraser.

Tie-dye fabrics using various methods.
(*Clockwise from left*)
   Elastic bands
   Knotting
   Tying
   Pegging
(*Centre*)
   Twisting

TIE-DYEING

Tie-dye or tie-dyeing is a resist-dyeing process. It consists of knotting, binding, folding or sewing parts of the fabric in such a way that, when it is dyed or painted, the dye cannot penetrate certain areas. After dyeing, the bindings are removed to reveal the undyed areas in the form of patterns. A great variety of different designs can be created depending on the method of tying, pegging or binding. The end results can be predicted to a certain extent, but there is always a surprise when the bindings are removed.

With the wide range of fabric paints now on the market, you do not even need to dye the fabric in a bucket but can simply spray, squirt or dribble the paints on to the material.

Equipment needed

- Fabrics
- Dyes and paints
- String, elastic bands, sewing thread, pegs, stones
- Bucket, tray, spray bottles, droppers
- Newspaper, plastic sheeting

Fabrics

Natural fibres such as cotton and silk, and also rayon ('artificial' silk made from cellulose), give the best results. Part-polyester fabrics will work, but the colours will be paler because synthetic fabrics do not take the dye. Try tie-dyeing cotton T-shirts for some dramatic results. Wash the fabric first to remove any size.

Dyes

Procion fibre-reactive dyes work really well. The dye will not fade, even after years, as it actually bonds to the fabric with a chemical reaction. Some wonderful results can also be obtained with fabric paints.

Ties

String, buttonhole thread, quilting thread, plastic twine, raffia, elastic bands and pipe-cleaners can all be used for binding the fabric. You can coat the string with a layer of wax by pulling it across a candle, to make it waterproof.

Pegs and bulldog clips can be used to clamp the fabric and marbles, stones, beads and buttons can be used to tie into the material. The fabric can be tied, sewn, draped, knotted or pegged in many different ways, as described below.

Twisting and coiling
Twist the fabric until it coils on itself. Bind or knot at each end or along the length at regular intervals.

Circles
Pick up the centre of the fabric and fold it into a cone shape. Bind the fabric down the length of the cone. Small circles will be

Twisting and knotting

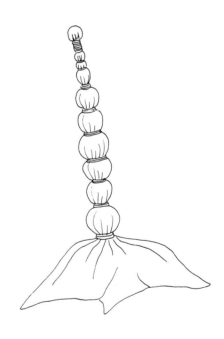

Tying circles

formed near the point; outer ones will be larger.

Marbling
Simply scrunch up the fabric into a huge ball and tie it up.

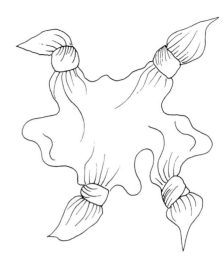

Tying circles around stones

Knotting corners

Pleating, draping and folding
Gather the fabric, pleat or fold it, drape it in spirals or crumple it. It can be folded diagonally, vertically or horizontally. If you are going to use the squirt-on method you sometimes don't even need to bind it (see the T-shirts in the photograph overleaf). You can also see some of these methods on page 66.

Knotting
Tie knots along the length of the fabric, or in each corner, either to form a cone or at random.

Sewing
Gather the fabric with a sewing thread. This can be done by hand or on a machine. Many shapes can be made with this method (see the T-shirts in the photograph overleaf).

Ruching
Gather the fabric around a piece of wood, a pencil or some tubing and bind to form a resist stripe.

Pegging
Fold the fabric and, using pegs or bulldog clips, clamp at intervals.

Dyeing

There are three ways in which you can dye your fabric: by submerging it in a dyebath; by dipping it in dye and then soaking it in a plastic bag; or by painting, squirting or spraying it with fabric paints.

Submerging fabric in a dyebath
All fabric-dye manufacturers will have their own recipes, so follow the instructions on the tin

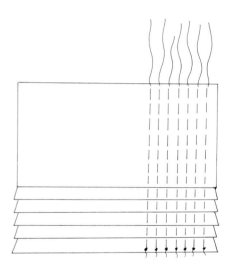

Sewing fabric for gathering

or packet. For Procion dyes, which are quite brilliant, use 15 g (½ oz) of dye to 450 g (1 lb) of fabric, three gallons (13·5 litres) of water and 50 g (2 oz) of soda-ash fixer.

Dissolve the dye in 300 ml (½ pint) of warm water and then add three gallons (13·5 litres) of lukewarm tap water. Stir. Add the fabric or T-shirts and stir constantly for fifteen to twenty minutes. Dissolve 50 g (2 oz) of soda-ash fixer in 575 ml (one pint) of hot water and add this to the bath. Do not pour soda ash directly on to the fabric. Remove the fabric and rinse it. Make sure that your bucket or dyebath is large enough: if the fabric cannot move freely, streaks and blotches will result. When the fabric is dry, you can of course add more bindings and dye another colour.

This method of tie-dyeing can cause some disappointments. When untying your work, you may find that the dyes have seeped under the bindings and that you are left with not much of a pattern, or with an all-over one-colour fabric. To prevent this, make sure that your bindings are really tight.

Instead of leaving the fabric in a dyebath for twenty minutes, you can place it in a microwave oven, in a shallow dyebath, for five minutes. Only small pieces can be dyed in this way.

The following recipes for dyeing are perfect and the results are almost guaranteed, which is wonderful when you have a class of enthusiastic ten-year olds all eager to undo their string and discover what they have created!

Soak method

Dissolve the dye in 575 ml (one pint) of warm water. Use between 30 and 90 ml (two and six tablespoons) of dye, depending on how deep you require the colour, plus 15 ml (one tablespoon) of urea. Dissolve 10 ml (two teaspoons) of soda ash in 300 ml (½ pint) of hot water. Mix these two solutions together and dip in your fabric, immersing it completely and making sure that the dye has penetrated. Squeeze out the material immediately afterwards to remove the excess dye.

If you are using the squirt-on paint method, you can soak the fabric first in the soda ash and water. Then paint on your dyes using as many colours as you wish.

Place the fabric inside a polythene bag or cover it in clingfilm; it needs to stay wet. Leave it for at least eight hours so that the chemical reaction can take place. Remove, rinse and then untie the bindings.

Painting on, squirting and spraying

Fabric paints and direct painting-on dyes can be used to spray, squirt, drop or dribble paint on to the fabric. You can use spray bottles, eye-droppers or just squeeze the dye from a bottle.

This method is very quick, and you can pleat, swirl, crumple and drape the fabric, as well as using the more traditional tie-dye binding methods. Try a test first to see how far the dye will spread on your fabric. If it spreads too far, thicken it. Wait until it is dry and heat-fix the paint by ironing, or in a tumble-drier.

Discharge paste and bleach can also be painted on to previously dyed fabrics.

Sunshine-bright T-shirts using the tie-dye squirt-on method

GUTTA

The gutta, or serti, technique involves drawing fine lines of gutta on to the fabric to outline the design. These lines act as a resist and stop the dyes from spreading into each other. Liquid dyes are painted directly on to the fabric and fixed into it.

There is also a variety of other ways of applying gutta to create imaginative textures and designs.

Equipment needed

- Fabric
- Gutta and solvent
- Nibs, pipettes and cone
- Dyes
- Frame and pins
- Brushes and applicators
- Hairdryer

Fabrics

Gutta resist is most effective on silk, but can also be used on wool and lightweight cottons.

Types of gutta

There are two types of gutta: solvent-based and water-based. Water-based gutta has the advantage of being removable from the fabric simply by washing and is safe for children to use. Solvent-based gutta needs to be removed by dry-cleaning or washing in white spirit. Some professionals swear by solvent-based gutta, as it always produces a consistent, very clear line (you can paint on it when dry or up to it when wet and it still works).

You can buy the gutta in containers with their own spouts, or you can pour it into a pipette and fix on a metal nib.

Fabrics painted with gutta.
(*From left to right*)
Gutta swirls on a pre-painted background
A black-gutta outline highlights the world map
Several different-sized nibs and gutta applicators were used to vary the width of line in this design
Gutta dripped and painted on as a textured resist
Anti-spread painted on to a tiny world-map picture
Gutta dropped and swirled on to a wet, painted background

Should the gutta be too thick, water or solvent can be added to thin it. Water-based gutta can become soggy if dyes are painted over it, and some guttas go rather gooey if they are steam-fixed. Solvent-based guttas do not create these problems, but they do suffer from evaporation and thickening. Try various guttas and decide which one suits you.

Coloured and metallic guttas

Coloured and metallic guttas remain in the fabric. Some of these types of guttas should not

be dry-cleaned or they will disappear, but the new permanent guttas will remain in the fabric even after dry-cleaning. Metallic guttas are more expensive, but are very effective and can add sparkle and create an interesting surface texture. Sometimes they can clog the nib which can be frustrating; if this happens, try using a larger nib. Do not use the ordinary metallic guttas on an article which is to be washed frequently, as it does tend to rub off with time.

Coloured guttas are available in all colours. You can also make your own by adding stained-glass colour, typographic ink or certain silk dyes to clear gutta. To make your own coloured gutta, mix a small amount of colour with the appropriate thinning agent (water or solvent) and then add it to clear gutta. Do not dry-clean fabric which contains home-made coloured gutta.

Nibs, pipettes and cones

Gutta is stored in its own applicator, complete with spout,

(*Opposite*)
Superbly coloured scarves, decorated with ideas from all over the world.
(*Top left*) India: silver and black gutta with texture created using a chamois leather
(*Top right*) Russia: bright babushkas using black gutta
(*Bottom left*) Britain: a country garden made with clear gutta
(*Bottom right*) USA: Indian chief created with clear gutta

or it can be decanted from a larger bottle into a plastic pipette. A waxed paper cone, rather like a home-made icing bag, can also be used. The thickness of the gutta line depends very much on the size of the cone or spout opening. A fine needle can pierce the spout to obtain a medium-sized line, or a neater, finer line can be achieved by attaching a nomographic nib to the spout.

Nibs are available in different sizes from no. 4 to no. 10 (the lower the number, the finer the

hole). Different makes of nib have different methods of fixing: they can be attached to the spout or the pipette with masking tape, screw on, or be slotted inside the top of the pipette. The nib comes supplied with a fine wire which should be kept to unblock the hole should it become clogged. You can aid drying time of the gutta with a hairdryer.

Making a cone from greaseproof paper

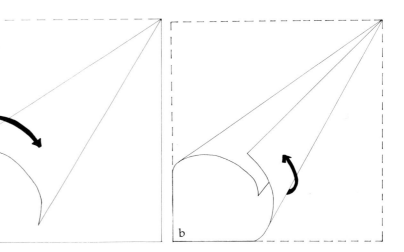
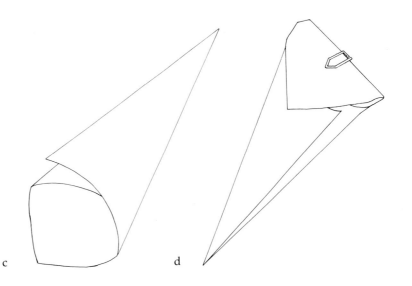

43

Dyes

Silk-painting dyes and paints are ideal for this technique. Fabric dyes mixed up for painting direct can also be used. Some fabric paints work well, too, but may need to be thinned. Take care not to use too much dye and flood the area, or the lines of resist created by the gutta will be broken down. The drying of the dyes can be aided with a hairdryer.

Step-by-step gutta technique. First, coloured gutta is applied using a pipette and nib

TRADITIONAL GUTTA

Application of gutta

Decide first on the colour of gutta and the thickness of the line you require. Stretch the fabric on to a frame, transfer the design on to the fabric and assemble the gutta, pipette and nib. Holding the pipette like a pen, test the flow of gutta on a scrap of paper and then squeeze steadily and gently so that the gutta flows, forming a continuous line around your design.

Check that the gutta has penetrated the fabric by looking on the back or holding it up to the light. If you work too fast, you will end up with breaks in the line. It is useful to keep a tissue in your hand as you work, as excess gutta sometimes collects around the nib. If you find that your line is too thick and uneven with a thick blob at the start and finish, your nib is too large; replace it with a smaller one. If you smudge or accidentally mark your work with gutta, place a folded tissue under the area and rub gently using a cotton bud dipped in gutta solvent.

Application of dyes

When the gutta is dry, start by painting the paler colours first.

You will be able to check for any leaks of dye seeping over, under or through your gutta line. Keep your gutta-filled pipette ready to use in emergencies, such as blocking holes or adding motifs to the design to cover up mistakes. Never overload your brush as a little goes a long way. The dyes must be worked into the fibres of the material.

When shading, paint lighter colours first, and then introduce the darker tones while the dye is still wet. When painting large areas and backgrounds, speed is essential or watermarks will appear, especially on silk. Large foam brushes and cotton wool can be used.

If spots of dye accidentally spill on to the unpainted area of your fabric, you can try to remove them using water or alcohol. If this is not successful, use some creative flair and change your design to incorporate the accident as part of a new design. You could also paint over the whole area and 'salt texture' it (see page 17). When you have finished painting and your work is dry, fix the dyes into the fabric using the appropriate method.

Gutta does not have to be used just as an outliner on fabric. Remember that it is a resist, and can be used in a variety of ways.

The dyes are applied, and the flowers shaded

Gutta painted on a wet background

Gutta poured on to a wet, painted background produces interesting results. The paint underneath a water-based gutta will turn paler. Solvent-based gutta lines will spread out over the dye, rather like petrol on water.

Brushing on gutta

Use old brushes, not your best fabric-painting brushes for this.

45

The finished gutta flower-and-flag cushion-cover

Apply gutta using a brush and then apply dyes. You can also use the gutta for adding definition once you have applied the dyes and they are dry.

Dribbling and flicking gutta

Flick large blobs of gutta on to the fabric and tilt the frame to let the gutta run down. Tilt and turn the frame at will. If the gutta is too thick, add some

solvent. This is a useful way of using up old gutta, the shelf life of which has run out.

Sponging on the gutta

Gutta can be applied to the fabric using a sponge or rags to create texture. Apply dyes by spraying or with a brush.

Adding solvent to gutta

Gutta can still retain its impenetrable property but becomes much more liquid if some solvent is added. Dilute the gutta – three parts gutta to two parts solvent – and apply it

to the fabric. When dyes are applied, a second layer of clear resist forms around the gutta line. This only works with solvent-based guttas.

Anti-spread

An anti-spread is available for water-based gutta, or gutta can be diluted with its solvent and spread over the surface of the fabric to create an anti-spread. This will prevent the dyes from spreading, enabling you to paint directly on to the fabric without the dye penetrating. The higher the proportion of gutta, the more resistant the fabric

The gutta technique was used to outline the flower-and-leaf design on these pretty hat bands

becomes to the dye. If you use a very high proportion of gutta, the effect will be like trying to paint on a waterproof surface, and will create a spotty, random texture.

SUGAR

Sugar in solution can act as a resist. This works very well on silks and fine cotton, especially with steam-fixed dyes. Granulated sugar can be sprinkled on wet fabric, which causes dye to move away from the granules. Granulated sugar can also be mixed into a solution. When icing sugar is used in a thick syrup solution, however, dramatic effects are created, as the sugar syrup acts as a resist.

Fabric is painted with the thick syrup solution and then dyes are added. The solution acts as a resist and tries to stop the dyes spreading. It is not an absolute barrier like wax or gutta, so the dye slowly creeps in and around the sugar syrup, creating a softer edge. As the fabric dries, the dyes are pushed away from the sugar, creating some wonderful textures which can resemble biological cells, marbled effects and galaxies.

The textures formed are created by the interaction of the sugar, water, dyes and fabric. The end result will be different every time, depending on how thick the syrup is, how wet the fabric is and how quickly it dries.

Equipment needed

- Fabric
- Icing and granulated sugar
- Frame and pins
- Dyes and water
- Brushes and applicators

Icing sugar

Icing sugar is ideal for making syrup solution. Mix equal quantities of icing sugar and water, and boil the mixture until it is reduced by half. The solution needs to be fairly thick with the syrup-like consistency of double cream. It can be used hot or cold. The solution can be stored in an airtight container in the fridge for several weeks. After a time it will go solid, but it can be re-heated and made ready for use again, so it does not go to waste.

Granulated sugar

You can also make a solution of granulated sugar and lukewarm water. Mix one litre (1¾ pints) of water to 250 g (9 oz) of sugar. A solution will form immediately, and this can be painted over the whole piece of fabric. When the dyes are painted on this, they do not immediately spread as the sugar granules act as a resist or anti-spread. A crusty texture is formed, which is useful for sand and earth pictures.

Fabrics painted using sugar syrup and granules as a resist.
(*Clockwise from top left*)
   Granules on brown satin
   Wide-brush flowers
   Resist squeezed through a pipette for
   geometric shapes
   Stiff hand-brush stripes
   Random dripping and trickling

USING SYRUP SOLUTION

To use the syrup solution, stretch the fabric on to a frame. Protect the table beneath from syrup blobs, as when they dry they are hard to remove. Drop the solution from a brush or dropper, squeeze it from a bottle or apply it with an assortment of brushes. While the sugar is still wet, apply dyes until the whole piece of fabric is painted, unless of course you plan to leave some areas unpainted. You can also use a spray to cover the fabric with dye. Dyes can be applied when the sugar is dry, and a much firmer resist edge will then form, but more interesting results will develop if you paint while the solution is still wet.

The syrup can also be spattered, flicked and dribbled on to the fabric. You can draw with it or print it on with a sponge. Try tilting the frame so that the syrup and dyes trickle down the fabric.

The fabric may take up to two or three days to dry. After a while, when the dyes have stopped reacting, you can dry the fabric with a hairdryer.

USING SUGAR SOLUTION

Stretch the fabric and paint the granulated-sugar solution on to the background. Leave this to dry, and then paint on the dyes.

The solution takes some time to dry and it is difficult to remove the crystals. Sometimes they look quite effective left on the fabric, especially in a sea or beach scene.

Fixing

When fixing these fabrics, you will need to use at least a double layer of fixing paper. It is sticky and messy, as the sugar solution runs out of the fabric and on to the fixing paper. Be sure to wash all the sugar solution out of the fabric after fixing.

Painting dye around sponged sugar resist

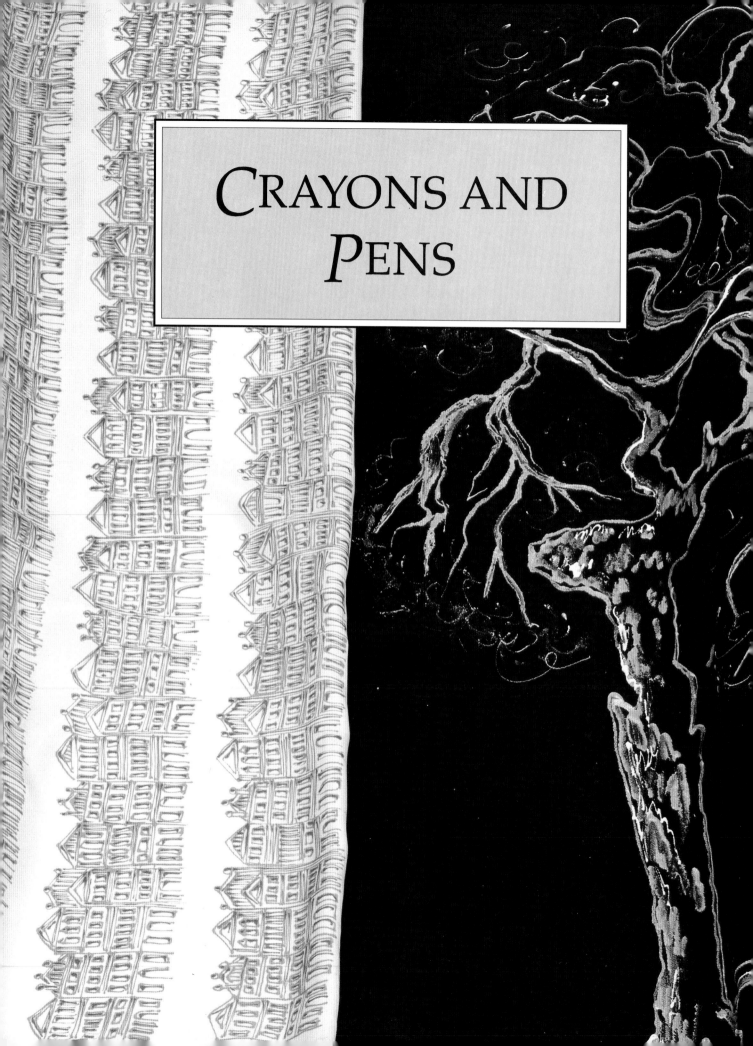

CRAYONS AND PENS

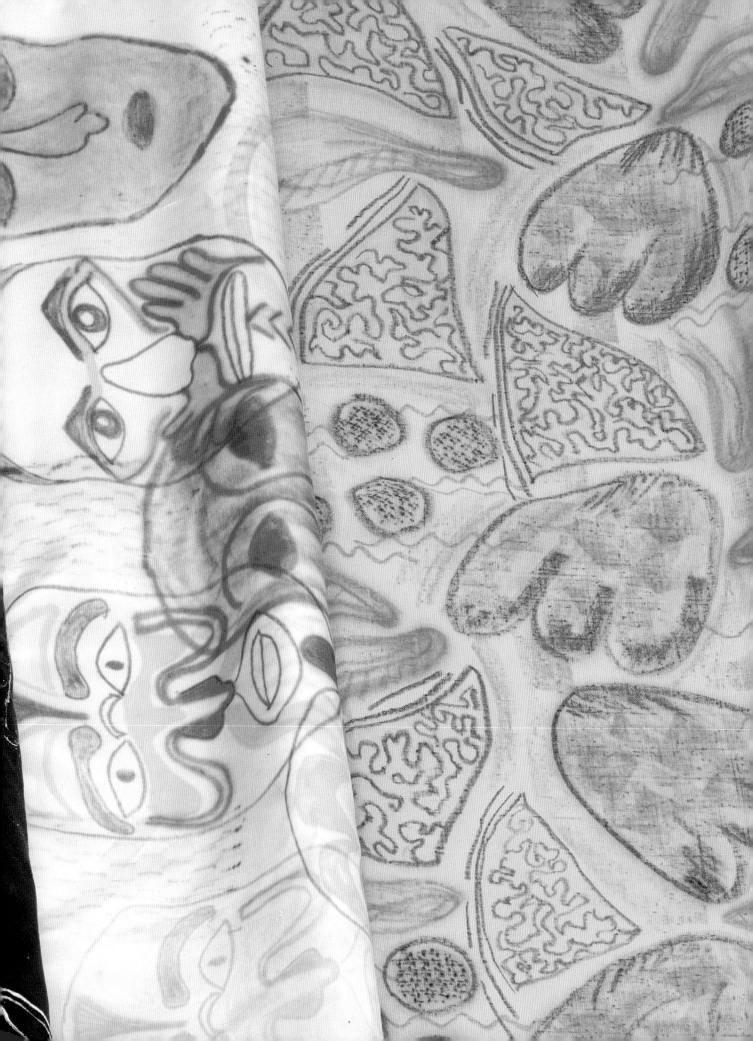

Art and craft shops are bursting with tubes, pens and bottles containing fabric colours. These are becoming increasingly popular for quick, instant decoration of clothing, cards, pictures and household items. We have produced a wealth of examples to give you ideas on their uses. They may be combined with other techniques, stretching their own limitations to create more texture and highlighting on your work.

Equipment needed

- Fabric
- Pastels, crayons
- Transfer crayons
- Foil, glue
- Glitter, puffa, fluorescent, pearlized, outliner pens
- Permanent marker pens
- Frame and pins
- Paper
- Iron
- Hairdryer

Crayons

There are three types of crayons on the market:

- transfer crayons
- steam-fixed crayons
- iron-fixed crayons

The crayons are made up of a combination of wax and pigment, and resemble children's wax crayons.

Fabrics

Unless the fabric you are using is thick, the crayons will drag on the surface. We have therefore found it easier to stretch the fabric on to a frame before crayonning, or an alternative would be to tape it to a table.

The texture of the fabric is important. A rough bourette, for example, would produce a more textured effect than crayonning on a smooth satin. Experiment with wild silk or hessian for unusual results.

(Below)
Some of the equipment needed, with fabric samples.
(From left to right)
   Black georgette with metal-foil rose-and-leaf motif
   Green landscape on a linen background, made with a variety of puffa pens, outliners and surface decorators
   Wild silk with an abstract design, showing the variety of textures produced with outliners, glitter pens and marker pens
   Brass-rubbing can be fun, using fabric crayons as the medium
   A striking pattern in gold-and-silver felt-tip marker pen on a green background; these pens are available in many widths

(Previous page)
Samples showing the range of effects which can be achieved using different techniques.
(From left to right)
   White pongée decorated with black-and-gold fabric-marker pen; ideal for architectural designs
   Dark, rich velvet with a raised textural tree form created with puffa pens and outliners
   Dramatic mask designs on polyester, illustrating effectively the repeat printing of transfer-crayon designs
   Iron-fixed crayon on linen, used to enhance the fabric with subtle textures

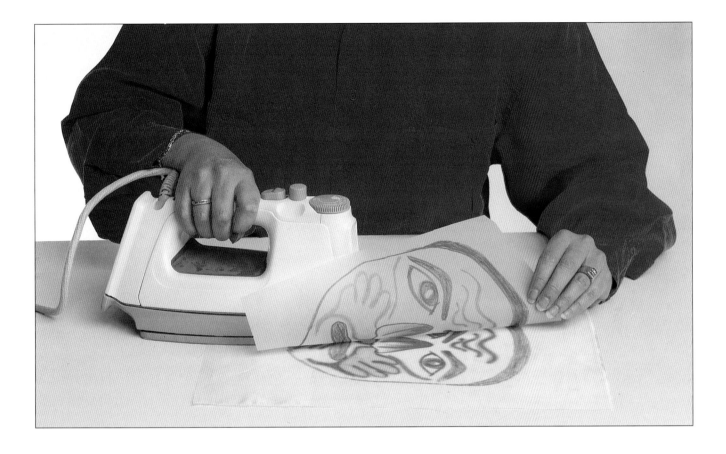

TRANSFER CRAYONS

These crayons can only be used on man-made fabrics such as polyester or synthetic blends. They become amazingly bright when transferred by ironing from paper to fabric. Always colour-test first with the crayons, as the heat of the iron alters the colours considerably. When used on natural fibres, they are paler and more indistinct.

● Firmly draw your design with the crayons on to white paper. Remember that, when ironed, the design will be reversed. Brush away any unwanted specks of crayon or these could be printed on to the fabric.

● Lay some paper on your ironing-board and then place the fabric on top. If you are ironing on to a garment, insert sheets of paper between the back and front to prevent the crayon from printing through to the underside.

● Lay your design face-down on the fabric and protect it with another sheet of white paper. Heat the iron to the 'cotton' setting and iron carefully and firmly over the whole design. Continue pressing until you see a slight imprint on the top sheet of paper.

● Remove the paper to reveal your design. The crayon colours will have changed and become

A wax transfer-crayon design being ironed on to man-made fabric

extremely vibrant. Try using a design two or three times, repeating the pattern or over-printing; it will fade each time you iron but will produce interesting, three-dimensional effects.

● The fabric is machine-washable in warm water. Do not tumble-dry.

STEAM-FIXED CRAYONS

Steam-fixed crayons can be used with dyes as a resist as well as on their own. When the crayon is melted into fabric with a hairdryer, the wax outline forms a barrier which can be painted around.

• Stretch the fabric on to a frame. We have found that fine fabrics such as pongée and cotton work well. Crayon on the surface, making sure that no gaps are left or dye will leak through when it is painted later on.

• Heat the fabric carefully with a hairdryer until all the wax is melted. Allow the fabric and wax to cool. The work is then ready to paint.

• Paint carefully with the dye. Take care not to overload the surface, or the barrier may not hold. Try not to paint over the crayon with dye, as some of the colour will be absorbed and the clarity of the wax outline will be spoiled. The resisting edges of the crayons are often encroached by the dyes, giving a textured line.

• Steam the fabric carefully to fix the crayon, using a double piece of paper to prevent re-printing.

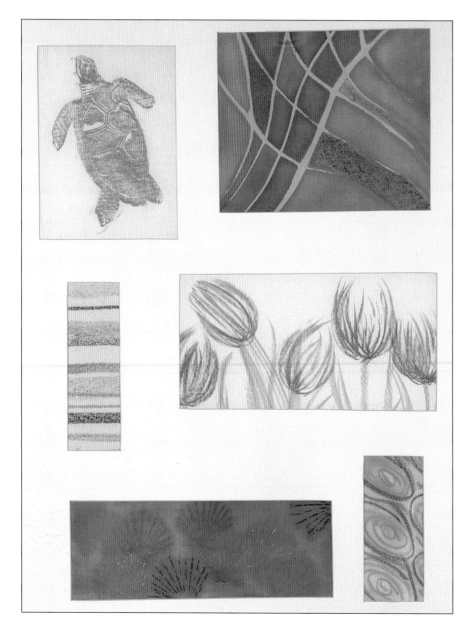

(*Opposite*)
Glamorous eveningwear.
(*From left to right*)
    Huge fringed evening shawl decorated with star constellations in gold-glitter and silver-felt-tip marker pens
    An Oriental flavour is created with this dramatic Chinese-dragon design on bodice and sleeve, along with a stylish use of glitter, black-felt-tip marker pen and gold outliner
    A superb, sheer, floor-length shawl decorated with glitter pens depicting sun-god motifs

(*Left*)
Crayon sample sheet.
(*Top, left and right*)
    Blue-turtle wax-crayon rubbing
    Steam-fixed-crayon pattern melted to form a resist for dyes. Flower texture-rubbing enhances some of the plain-coloured areas
(*Centre, left and right*)
    Thick silk bourrette textured with fabric-crayon stripes
    Transfer-crayon tulips
(*Bottom, left and right*)
    Purple-painted background and rubbings in wax over fan-shaped shells
    Silk painted with lively swirls

IRON-FIXED CRAYONS

Iron-fixed crayons do not spread like steam-fixed crayons, so they do not create an effective barrier to dye. This does not mean, however, that they cannot be used with dyes. Painting fabric with background colours and highlighting with crayons can be attractive.

● These crayons become permanent in the fabric when ironed. Place sheets of paper over and under the fabric surface on the ironing-board and iron on the 'cotton' setting for two to three minutes.

● When using these crayons with steam-fixed dyes, iron the fabric before steaming.

● Create textures by rubbing over surfaces with the crayons. Anything with a distinct surface texture can be used, such as bark, leaves, grass or grit (natural), or graters, plastic lids, string, placemats, doilies, lace and nets (man-made). Place the objects on a flat surface and tape the fabric firmly over the top. Gently rub over the surface,

55

Evening accessories for that special occasion. The satin evening purse has a metal-foil design, machine-quilted and beaded for a textured effect. The hair accessories, bow and clasps are prettily patterned with bright, sparkling glitter pens, along with original clasp ear-rings to make an evening outfit complete

trying not to smudge the delicate effects. Alternatively, stretch your fabric on to a frame to keep it taut.

● Rub the crayons themselves over lace or leaves and then iron these on to your fabric to print the textures.

● Experiment with making marks on the fabric using the crayons. Create different intensities of colour by stippling, rolling, twisting and scoring the crayons.

FOIL

Add glamour to your fabric by using the special sheet-foil paper available at silk-painting suppliers (see pages 126–7). We have found it rather expensive to use and have discovered that, on large surfaces, it is difficult to make it adhere permanently, but the effect is worth the trouble taken. Black fabrics reflect the metallic sheen of the gold and silver, or it can richly enhance jewel-bright silk-painting dyes.

There are two ways of sticking the foil on to the fabric: using a glue substance from a tube, or a rubbery solution from a bottle.

Tube

Dab the fabric using the glue pen or tube, then place the foil

paper on top and rub hard with a firm object such as a coin. Carefully lift off the foil paper. The foil will adhere to the glue.

Bottle

Apply the rubbery liquid to the fabric through the bottle nozzle. Allow it to dry without smudging. Place the foil on top of the hard lines and iron with a fairly hot iron. The rubber substance will melt and attach itself to the foil. Peel off the backing paper gently to reveal the fabric.

FABRIC PENS

Fabric pens are dye-filled felt-tip pens. They come in three different sizes: thin, medium and thick. They do not show up on dark-coloured fabric, but are extremely useful for detailed linear work, intricate patterns and small areas. They often need to be re-applied to increase the dye intensity, but, once fixed, they are fade-resistant and machine-washable. They are fixed into the fabric by ironing on the wrong side with a hot iron. Many brands are refill-able, and new fibre tips can be bought. This is a great advantage, as we have found that they dry out quickly and are extremely short-lived when used for colouring in large areas. The colour range is small, but you can create more shades by over-painting.

Some pens will blend when a wash of water is applied, giving the effect of a watercolour painting. When using fabric pens to highlight a piece of work that has been painted with dyes or paints, fix the work first and then add the felt-tip pens. Fix the pens afterwards.

PERMANENT MARKER PENS

These pens work with a pumping action and are generally available in black, gold

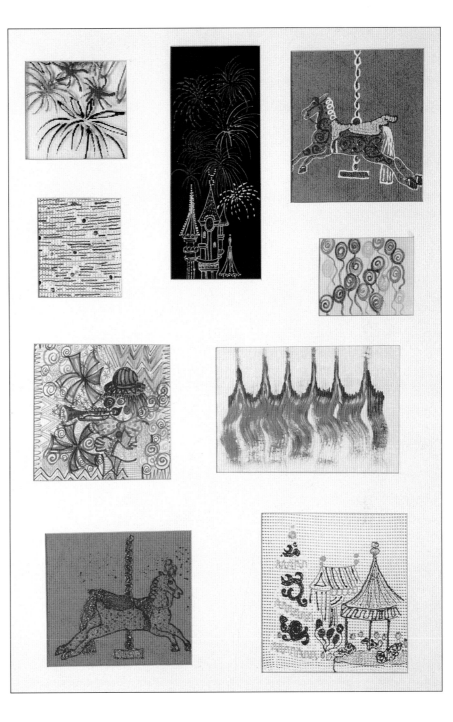

A sample sheet of felt-tip marker pens, puffa pens, outliners and glitter pens.
(*Left, from top to bottom*)
    Flower fantasy on net, cut away within the outliner-resist shapes
    Painted fluorescent background with linear texturing of glitter and outliner pens on embroidery fabric
    Fantasy fun with felt-tip pens
    Merry-go-round horse on felt, with fluorescent patterns in puffa pen, glitter pens and outliners
(*Centre, top*)
    Dramatic Disney skyline on black satin, created with paint-writer, scribble and three-dimensional outliner pens
(*Right, from top to bottom*)
    Fluorescent fairground using glitter and puffa pens and outliners on a felt background
    Bright balloons on poly/cotton, made with permanent marker pens
    Making waves with puffa pens: scallops of colour placed on top of one another, scraped downwards and then hairdried to puff
    Puffa pens, glitter pens and outliners were combined in this fairground sample

and silver. The liquid comes out of the tip – sometimes in a rush – so check the flow on paper before applying it to your fabric.

Very fine black markers are ideal for outlining, signing your work and adding definition.

Gold and silver markers look most effective on black or dark fabrics. Although washable, we would suggest testing the make carefully as the qualities do vary. Iron on the back of the fabric with a hot iron to fix.

OUTLINERS
(puffa, glitter, fluorescent and pearlized pens)

There are now many brands of outliners available for fabric painting. They can be used on most fabrics, but do check the manufacturers' instructions. Puffa pens tend to pucker fine weights of fabric.

These outliners come in tubes or bottles, and are often called surface-decoration pens. They produce a raised line which looks like wet plastic, which, when dry, adheres to the fabric. The technique is sometimes known as liquid embroidery. We have had great fun decorating items from baseball caps to canvas boots.

Outliners are effective in fluorescent and pearlized colours and will brighten up any plain fabric. They are sometimes thick enough to form a barrier, rather like gutta, and dyes can be painted in and around them. There is a tendency for them to stick on to the paper when steam-fixing. This can be avoided if you unroll the paper while it is still hot.

Outliners sit on the surface of the fabric, and therefore have a very definite right and wrong side. They dry with a rubbery feel and in some cases will need to be ironed on the wrong side to fix into the fabric.

The amazing puffa pens, when dry, are expanded using a hairdryer to produce a three-dimensional effect. They do not expand evenly, so care must be

taken to apply them with a similar thickness of line, although this characteristic may be used to advantage with landscapes or combined-technique work. If you wish,

attach a nomographic nib (no. 7–9) to the end of the tubes to control the flow a little better and produce a more even line. Glitter pens are certainly more successful when used in this way.

Brighten up Christmas Day with a collection of cheery clothes. Simple Christmas motifs add glitter and colour (made with puffa pens, glitter pens and outliners) to decorate caps, boots and cotton T-shirts

SPRAYING

Spraying is a wonderful technique for achieving textures on fabric. It is usually fast and creates movement and random colouring. The tones and colours can be built up from fine layers of dyes and paint, using an airbrush, to heavier spattering using a garden spray or toothbrush.

The thicker the fabric, the more effective the spray. Thinner fabrics, such as pongée 5, tend to absorb the dyes, although this can to a certain extent be altered by applying a layer of anti-spread to the silk before spraying.

Spraying is linked very much with stencilling, which is discussed in the following chapter. The fabric is often masked by a template in the form of a stencil, through which dye or paint is sprayed to create varying intensities of colour. Other ways of masking to create textures could be to use items such as lace, stones, cotton wool or masking fluid and film.

If the only requirement is to create textured backgrounds to your work, then the technique can be carried out very quickly

to produce vibrant surfaces, but the skill of using an airbrush will require a great deal of forethought and expertise. Do not be daunted by this, as the results will be stunning.

Equipment needed

Sprays
- Airbrush and compressor
- Air gun and compressed-air canister
- Eco-spray and compressed-air canister
- Diffuser (mouth diffuser or fixative sprayer)
- Air pump
- Garden spray or cleaning-product bottle
- Perfume atomizer
- Toothbrush, nailbrush or stiff brush
- Spray-paint canister

Stencil equipment
- Oiled card
- Acetate
- Cards
- Masking film or polyphane
- Sharp craft knife
- Cutting board
- Varnish

Other equipment
- Fabric
- Dyes and paints
- Diluent
- Anti-spread
- Newspaper, polythene sheeting
- Large sheets of cardboard
- Frame and pins
- Masking tape

- Brushes, palettes, applicators, jars
- Cotton wool
- Ruler, tracing paper
- Hairdryer

Preparation

Organizing the spraying area is very important. The fine spray mist of dye or paint can cover any surface, so make sure that you have plenty of polythene or newspaper around. A dry, windless day is ideal for spraying out of doors and is certainly preferable if using compressed-air canisters, as the gases in these are quite strong. Indoors, it is always advisable to wear a small face-mask to protect your nose and mouth, as inhaling the dye particles in a confined space is inevitable.

It is useful to prop up your frame with the stretched fabric against a door or wall. Using the large sheets of cardboard, try to construct a spray 'booth' to confine the mess of spraying. Remember to cover behind this area as well as the floor.

Fabrics

As already mentioned, the finer the fabric, the more easily liquid is absorbed. Spray each layer very lightly and allow the fabric to dry between each layer. The colours will move and run down the fabric if it is over-saturated. This will result in textures like those achieved with the painting-direct techniques, and may be just what you are looking for.

(*Previous page*)
Four effects of spraying on 'difficult' fabrics.
(*Clockwise from the top*)
Pale grey velvet sprayed through canvas mesh
Luxurious satin sprayed in soft stripes
A subtle lace effect on crêpe de Chine
Crumpled calico with two-tone spraying

Make sure, once again, that you are using the correct dye or paint for the fabric. Wash any fabric which may contain size, as size will prevent the colour from being absorbed properly.

Dyes and paints

All types of unthickened dyes or paints can be used, depending of course on the choice of fabric. Many special dyes for spraying on fabric are now available, and these dry quickly on the fabric. Experiment with the depth of colours. You will notice that sprayed colour is much lighter than when applied with a brush because the tiny dots of colour are obviously less intense, so mix your colours darker and stronger.

We have found that, after steam-fixing, the dyes do become more vibrant. The application of a layer of anti-spread on to the fabric surface will also alter the final sprayed colour after fixing; the tiny

Very different spray effects are achieved with the equipment shown below.
(*Clockwise from left*)
    Mouth diffuser
    Garden spray jet
    Airbrush
    Toothbrush used for spattering
    Eco-spray

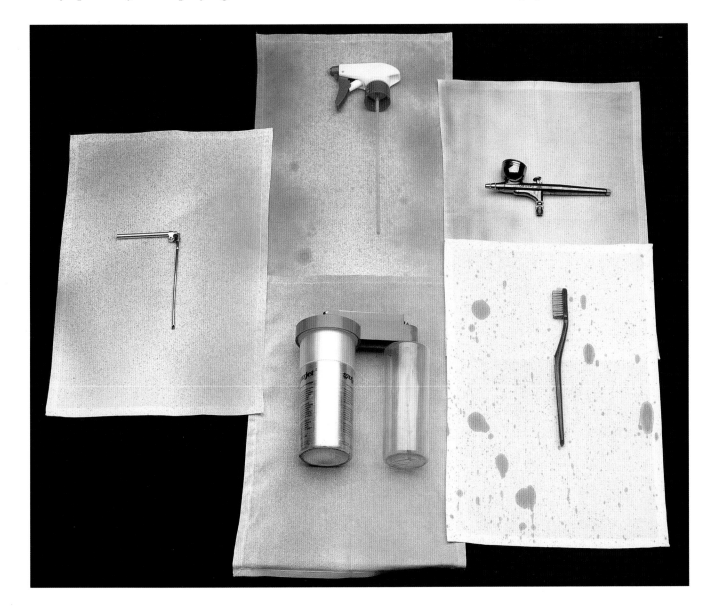

dye particles strengthen considerably. If the final colour is very important, then a test piece will need to be sprayed and fixed.

Car-spray paint gives excellent results, especially on cotton; it dries very quickly after each application of colour and fine layers of colour can be built up. The main disadvantage is that the spray stiffens the fabric and it loses its malleable quality.

Spray equipment

The finished spray effect depends very much on the fineness of the nozzle or applicator used to spray. Equipment can be varied from an old toothbrush to a state-of-the-art airbrush and compressor. Most of the samples shown in this chapter were made using an Eco-spray, mouth diffuser or airbrush.

Toothbrush

This is suitable when random spattering of colour is required. It is difficult to direct and obviously does not hold much paint, resulting in a patchy surface covering. A stiff brush is an ideal alternative.

Either use your finger to brush against the tip or draw a pencil across the tip. Vary the distance between the brush and fabric to alter the intensity of colour spattering. Remember to mask any area that you do not wish to be covered, as the spattering can travel a great distance!

Mouth diffuser

A mouth diffuser is a very useful piece of equipment. It is readily available in art shops. Simply place the longer pipe or tube into a jar of colour and sharply blow through the other, shorter pipe.

Try to begin your blow to one side of your work and quickly move the jet of spray colour across to the area you wish to cover. This will help to cut out the heavier dye particles which will come out of the tube when you begin to blow. Take care to

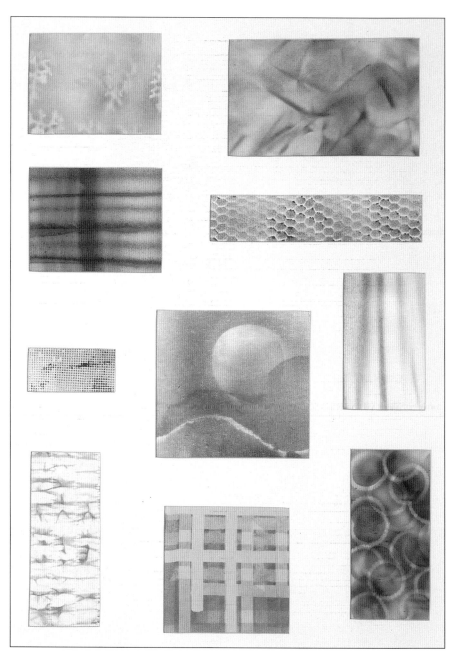

mask all areas that do not need spraying, and take your time with the diffuser; you will become quite light-headed if you blow for a period of time. We find the rough texture of the diffuser spray interesting when used on small areas or when sprayed through stencils.

Garden spray

Garden or household cleaning-product sprays produce a heavy jet of colour. Often this is just too random a technique, but it can be useful for graffiti work or on large background areas where big spots of colour are required. The pump action squirts the colour out in a dramatic fashion. It may be

---

(*Opposite*)
Spray sample sheet.
(*Top, left and right*)
    Aerosol-canister spray over foam shapes
    Crumpled crêpe with subtle shading
(*Second from top, left and right*)
    Pleating, spraying and re-pleating form a tartan effect
    Spraying over chicken wire on to cotton
(*Second from bottom, left to right*)
    Varying the intensity of spray through a mouth diffuser
    Airbrush technique over torn and cut paper masks
    Draping produces subtle shading on satin
(*Bottom, left to right*)
    Hand-gathered cotton with minimal spraying in two colours
    Masking-tape layers used to block spray
    Repeat spraying in three colours over plastic bangles, on crêpe de Chine

useful combined with the watercolour techniques of wet-on-wet or wet-on-dry (see pages 11 and 12).

Eco-spray and air gun

Eco-sprays and air guns give a much smoother covering of tiny dots, and the depth of colour can be controlled much more. Start spraying away from the fabric and bring the spray towards the area you wish to cover. When you finish, draw the spray away from the work to prevent heavy spattering when you release the pressure on the jet.

Airbrush

An airbrush has the great advantage of producing a very fine, subtle spray. Three-dimensional effects – spheres, boxes, drapery – can be created easily. The spray will not be textured, however, and you may feel that the work looks too planned and contrived. It depends very much on your projects and the atmosphere you wish to create. Should you wish to pursue the highly skilled airbrush technique, we suggest that you buy a detailed manual on the techniques.

The following ideas can be carried out using an Eco-spray, air gun and canister, mouth diffuser or spray can. It is not necessary to coat the fabric with anti-spread, although you may wish to do so on silk. Dry each layer of spray thoroughly before beginning another.

CRUMPLING (marbling)

Dampen the fabric slightly so that it will sit in a 'ball' shape. Spray the paint from one side. Re-arrange the creased shape and spray from the other side. Once again, re-arrange the fabric and spray from another direction. Speed up the drying time between the layers by using a hairdryer.

PLEATING AND GATHERING (controlled)

A very controlled striped effect can be created by folding the fabric in pleats and pinning at the edges to hold it in place. Spray lightly from one side on to the folds. Re-pleat and spray again, using another colour or shade, to create soft folds. If you wish to produce a checked or tartan effect, pin the fabric in the opposite direction before re-spraying.

PLEATING AND GATHERING (random)

Fold the fabric softly and attach it loosely in folds to a wooden frame using three-pronged pins. Direct the spray from different angles on to the fabric. The resulting colours will be varied in weight and texture, giving a lovely soft, striped effect.

PLEATING AND GATHERING (draped)

Pin the fabric on to the frame in a soft, draped effect. Catch up areas from behind and pin using dressmaking pins to create further creases and folds. Spray lightly from different directions, or re-pin and re-spray using a different colour or shade.

PLEATING AND GATHERING (hand or machine)

Using a fine thread, hand- or machine-gather the fabric loosely in broad bands. Draw it up into folds and place on a flat surface. Spray lightly over the gathers from two directions. Allow the fabric to dry, then remove the gathers and iron the fabric flat. An unusual texture is created, often resembling the results achieved by tie-dye (see pages 38–40). Additional gathers could be sewn and a second colour sprayed. A chequered effect can be produced in this way.

RESISTS (solid masks)

A very effective way of making patterns is to spray over shapes, re-position them and spray again. The shapes can be placed in a formal design or attached to the fabric at random. You will need either to pin the shapes or lightly spraymount them on to the fabric, as the frame must be tilted for the spray technique. Shapes cut out of masking film or polyphane will be slightly sticky already, and can simply be pressed on to the fabric. Remember to draw the shape on to the paper backing in reverse so that, when in position, the design is the correct way round.

When the shapes adhere to the background, a sharp, sprayed outline is created. If you peel back or raise part of the shape and spray over it, a more subtle, fuzzy effect is created. Experiment with these effects. The softer ones suggest distance

Luxurious nightwear and bedroom table, coloured using the spray technique

when used in a landscape; torn paper is most effectively used to suggest mountains and rolling hills.

RESISTS (found objects)

Use leaves, grasses, cow parsley or feathers as resisting shapes. Choose objects with a definite outline which will be effective when sprayed over. Attach the shapes by pinning, or spraymount them. We have also attached objects by painting them with masking fluid to hold them in place; after spraying the fluid can be rubbed away.

RESISTS (tape and liquids)

Masking tape is useful as a resist, as it can be easily stripped off the fabric after spraying. Stretch the fabric tightly, then press the tape on to the surface. Place additional strips on top of each layer of sprayed colour to resist more and more of the dye or paint. Dry the fabric and tape thoroughly before removing the tape to reveal the stripes.

Masking fluid can be used successfully to build up textures. Some fabrics may absorb the fluid, however, making rubbing away afterwards difficult, so test the fabric first. Apply the fluid lightly with a brush or dab it on with a sponge. Leave it to dry, and then spray over the surface.

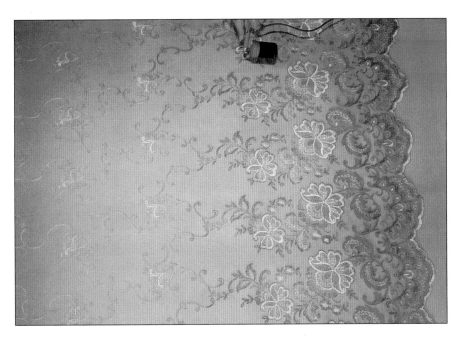

Add extra depth to your work by applying more fluid and repeating the spraying with the same or a different colour. Overlap the masking fluid to create varied tones. Remove the fluid by rubbing it away with your fingers.

SPRAYING THROUGH SHAPES

This technique is great fun, as the objects which you try to spray through will give you unexpected and unusual results. Household objects such as graters, grills and strainers can be used, and fabrics with an open weave, or the open designs of lace, are ideal.

The traditional way of cutting stencils is discussed in detail in the following chapter (see pages 72–3). Once prepared, a stencil is

Spraying colour through lace stretched over a frame

a quick way of covering fabric with designs and texture.

Either use anti-spread on your fabric, or leave it unprepared. Place the objects or fabric over the material which has been pre-stretched on a frame. Areas which are not covered, such as the tiny holes in lace or graters, will be coloured by the spray. Remember to cover over any areas which you do not wish to be covered with dye or paint with spare paper. The contrast achieved between the hard edges and background will create dramatic effects. Do not be afraid to re-position items and re-spray to create more depth.

STENCILLING

This simple technique may remind you of your schooldays: painting through simple shapes on punched-out card. The method is still the same, but the designs can be more intricate and the depth of shading more varied. The materials for stencilling are widely available, as the art form is enjoying renewed popularity, and craft shops stock a wide range of pre-cut designs and paints. Even if you feel that your drawing skills are limited, with this technique even simple designs can look extremely professional, especially when repeated.

(Right)
Stencilling equipment with examples of the results produced.
(From left to right)
   Fabric paint sprayed through a paper cut-out
   Oil-board flower design using car aerosol sprays
   Velvet teamed up with a geometric design
   Glitter pen and thickened paints used on warm-coloured silk

(Previous page)
Wonderful designs showing a variety of stencilled textures.
(From left to right)
   Art-deco design on cotton, using outliners and thickened dyes
   Dark linen with dramatic metallic-finish paints
   Screen and fabric paint sponged through a stencil design on to pre-sponged glazed cotton
   Subtle shades of oranges and leaves made with oil-based sticks
   Flying birds brushed over a cardboard template on to glazed cotton

Equipment needed

- Masking material: oiled manilla card, acetate, stencil paper, masking film
- Brushes: stencil brushes
- Sponges: natural and foam
- Paints: acrylic, textile, spray, dyes
- Crayons: specialist stencil, fabric
- Pencil, felt-tip pen
- Ruler
- Sharp craft knife
- Cutting-board or mat
- Tracing paper, carbon paper
- Masking tape, low-tack tape, spraymount
- Palettes, jars, saucers
- Frame and pins
- Anti-spread (antifusant)
- Thickener (Épaississant)
- Spray or mouth diffuser

Stencil paper (masking material)

Stencils must be cut from hardwearing, durable and flexible materials. Mass-produced, pre-cut stencils are usually made in transparent plastic. These are ideal, as you can see through the mask to position the stencil accurately. Some traditional, oiled-manilla card stencils are still found, which will have registration marks cut in them for lining up the design. The oiled card is easy to cut and wears well, but has the disadvantage of not being see-through.

If you are cutting your own stencils, try to buy clear acetate. Masking film used by airbrush painters could be used, but may not stick on to all fabrics and could curl away from the surface. Heavy paper or card is ideal for pieces of work which do not require repeated wetting with dye or paint, but it is not durable.

Cutting tools

A sharp cutting tool is needed to cut the stencil. Depending on the thickness of the stencil, you will need either a light craft knife or a heavy-duty Stanley knife. These have removable blades and are available at craft shops. It is important to have a sharp-pointed blade for cutting your stencil. A good cutting tool with a multi-blade is available. The tip of this can be snapped off when it has become blunt.

A metal ruler is also useful for cutting straight lines – a wooden ruler chips easily. Cut on a wooden board, or, if you intend to do a lot of stencilling, it may be worth investing in a special cutting-mat. These are excellent, as cutting does not mark the mat and the score on the surface re-seals.

Colouring equipment

There are many paints, sprays and crayons available for stencilling, but some may not be ideal for fabric. Read the manufacturer's instructions carefully.

Thickened iron-fixed fabric paints are ideal as they do not 'run' on the fabric. The colours will not creep under your template unless applied too thickly.

Aerosol-spray paints are very effective but will give a hard, stiff surface to the fabric.

Fabric dyes can be used with care. They are liquid and therefore saturate the fabric quickly. Use them with a spray gun or mouth diffuser. These have been discussed in detail in the previous chapter (see pages 63–4). Thicken up these dyes with thickener (épaississant) and then use them with a stencil.

Outliners, glitter pens and puffa paints have an ideal consistency for stencilling. We have used them with interesting textural results in some of our examples shown in this chapter. They will need to be ironed into

the fabric when dry to fix them, or expanded with a hairdryer.

Fabric crayons work well on most fabrics. If used directly, they are more effective within larger shapes, as the thickness of the stick prevents the colour from getting into corners. Specialist stencilling crayons which are applied with a brush produce extremely subtle results and are most effective. Check that they can be fixed properly into your fabric.

Brushes

Specialist stencilling brushes are often made from white china bristle. The bristles are cut across the tip to give the blunt end necessary when 'pouncing' the colours. Choose brush sizes suitable to your project, from 6–50 mm (¼–2 in). Small, detailed stencils will obviously require small brushes.

Sponges and fabric

Most stencillers use a brush to apply colour, but attractive textures can be created with a sponge. Natural sponges are soft and absorbent, with varied 'holes' which create textures. Foam sponges arranged or trimmed into rounded shapes produce a more even covering of colour. Shading, by applying more or less pressure, will enhance certain areas. Thick wool wrapped around your index finger can be dabbed through the cut designs.

Pre-sponged fabric is stretched using masking tape on to a printing pad. The stencil design is sponged through the template with fabric and screen-printing paint

Sprays

Refer to the previous chapter (see pages 64–5) for full descriptions of spraying equipment.

Positive stencil

Negative stencil

CUTTING THE STENCIL DESIGN

When choosing your design, keep your pattern simple, as it is difficult to cut very intricate patterns, even with a sharp knife. When a shape is cut from a stencil it must be attached to the outside or it will fall out. It can be attached by leaving a linking 'bridge' to the outside of the stencil.

Stencils can be positive or negative. A positive stencil is when the actual shape and design have been cut away. After stencilling, the masked background will remain unpainted and the cut-out shape will be painted. In a negative stencil, the background is cut away. After stencilling, the masked shape or design will remain unpainted and the cut-away background will be painted.

72

The simplest, or single, stencil gives you the whole design on one piece of card and is usually painted in one colour. A more complicated design may require a stencil for each part of it; these stencils would be laid on the fabric, one after the other, to build up the design and are known as multiple stencils. A modular stencil is one which has two or more motifs on one card; these can be placed wherever you like to build up a design.

1. Draw or trace your design on to the stencil card using a black marker pen.
2. Place the cutting-mat beneath the card and tape it firmly into place.
3. Hold the card firmly with one hand. Begin to cut the stencil with a sharp craft knife, away from your fingers. Keep the blade upright and try to cut smoothly. On thicker card, do not attempt to cut through in one go. Cut lightly at first and then go back and re-cut your lines. When cutting around shapes such as circles or flower petals, untape the stencil sheet and cut firmly, a little at a time, moving the stencil after each cut.

Sample stencilling sheet.
(*Top*)
    Airbrushing was used to create very subtle shading in this stunning flower design. Metallic powder was applied to the background as a wash
(*Centre, left and right*)
    One-colour stencil showing shading with oil-based stencil crayons
    Varied shading on a two-colour flower-and-leaf design
(*Bottom, left and right*)
    Warm tones react subtly on this velvet fabric
    Fabric textured by dry-brushing prior to stencilling

APPLYING THE COLOUR

Once the stencils have been cut, decide on the technique you will use: stencilling with a brush or spraying. Stencilling is ideal for small repeat motifs, whereas spraying is better on larger projects. The preparation of the worksurface is different for these techniques (see page 124).

1. Cover the worksurface with several layers of absorbent paper, and either stretch out the fabric and tape it firmly to the worksurface, or stretch the fabric tightly on to a frame and place it flat on the paper-covered worksurface.
2. Spraymount the stencil on to the stretched fabric or simply place on the stencil if you have used a sticky-backed paper such as masking film. Another method of attaching would be to use masking tape behind the stencil, although dye may creep beneath this.
3. Choose your paints, thickened dyes or crayon colour. Place on a palette or saucer and load the brush. Work off any excess paint on a piece of kitchen paper so that the brush is quite dry. Hold the brush rather like a pencil in an upright position and close to the bristles.
4. Apply the colour to the stencil cuts in one of two ways. Either jab, or 'pounce', the brush up and down to produce a textured, speckled effect, or gently use a circular motion from the outer edges of the stencil cut, building up the colour as you near the centre. The latter technique will give a much smoother, more blended effect. Add more colour to create shading, taking care not to overload the brush. Lift the stencil from time to time to see the effect of the colour.
5. Allow the fabric to dry thoroughly before placing multiple stencils on top of one another. Clean the undersides frequently to prevent stencils from smudging when replaced on the fabric in a repeat pattern.
6. Clean the stencil thoroughly and fix the paints into the fabric.

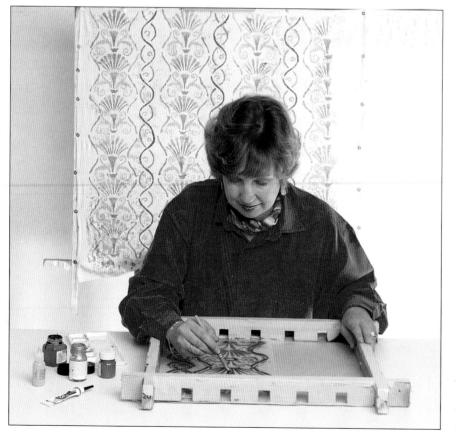

Dabbing through a cut-stencil design, with the fabric stretched taut on to a frame

USING TWO OR MORE COLOURS

The gradual building-up of colour and depth in your work will increase with experience. The three-dimensional quality in stencilling is important, and you can always add more colour to a piece of work when the first coat is dry. Never saturate the fabric, or bleeding under the template will occur.

If two or more colours are required on the same template, mask out the second colour area with masking tape and complete one colour first. Before you begin the second colour, you must let the first colour dry completely.

Stencilling on a previously painted background can produce exciting pieces of work. Try combining a rag-rolled or scumbling background with a stencil motif, or use metallic colours on a watercolour background.

Rich fabrics, such as velvet, reflect colours, creating even more luxurious depth of colour. Don't be afraid to stencil on a variety of textured and coloured fabrics to create unusual results.

A stunning pleated lampshade and a cloth, picking up the Chinese motif on the lamp. Two sponged and stencilled cushions bring all the colours together

PRINTING

We have included a chapter on printing techniques in this book, as we think you will find these techniques very useful for your surface-fabric decoration, especially if you need to produce long lengths of fabric. Hand painting is all very well on a square metre of fabric, but if you require ten metres you may find one of these methods a tremendous help. Mono-printing, for instance, can be a very good technique to use as a background, which can then be over-printed or painted on. Transfer-printing can be very useful for embroiderers as a background to their work, and screen-printing will enable you to print lengths of multi-coloured fabric in a short time.

Equipment needed

- Fabric
- Padded flat surface
- Paints
- Sheet of glass
- Screen and squeegee

- Saucers and paper
- Iron
- Rollers and brushes
- String, glue and card
- Lino- and wood-blocks
- Rubber stamps

Fabrics

All fabrics can be used to print on. Fabrics woven from natural fibres work best. Transfer-printing does work wonderfully on polyester, but can be carried out on natural fibres with a more subdued result. Be sure to wash the size out of the fabric or it will eventually fade after being painted.

Dyes and paints

Special paints are needed for transfer-printing, but most fabric paints can be used for other printing methods. They may need to be thickened. Opaque and metallic paints work well. Screen-printing and block-printing colours are made especially for screen- and block-printing, but most fabric paints and dyes can be used if you mix them with a thickener or binder. Try adding a little glycerine or washing-up liquid if you find that they dry up too quickly when you are trying to mono- or block-print.

Preparation

The fabric must be washed first and then ironed to get rid of the creases. Spread the fabric out on the padded printing table and tape it down. Some methods of printing will require a paint pad

---

Inks and dyes used for printing, with assorted samples of work

(*Previous page*)
Samples showing some of the many different printing techniques.
(*Top row, from left to right*)
  Rubber-stamp print
  Lemon print
  Photo-image print
  Wood-block print
  String print
(*Bottom row, from left to right*)
  Polystyrene-block print
  Lino print
  Glue print
  Transfer print
  Mono-print

for you to apply the dye, and for some techniques you will need a sheet of glass and a roller. A saucer with a layer of absorbent fabric (such as felt) or paper towels in which to soak the paints will make a dye pad.

FRUIT-, VEGETABLE-, PLANT- AND OBJECT-PRINTING

This is the simplest method of printing. Vegetables can be printed whole or with areas gouged out to form a design. Vegetables such as potatoes, turnips and carrots are good for cutting into, and broccoli and cauliflower florets can look like trees.

Objects such as nuts, bolts, feathers and even shoes can be printed. Parts of the body –

fingers, thumbs and footprints – can be used. Materials such as net, plastic wrapping, hessian or anything with a textured surface can make a print. Press flowers, leaves and grasses to use. All these plants and objects can simply be pressed on to your dye pad and then pressed or stamped on to the fabric.

STRING-PRINTING

Printing with string can create a drawn-line effect. Depending on the type of string you use – cord, fibrous or smooth string – different textures are created. Stick the string on a piece of stiff board in rows, coils or spirals. You can draw patterns or pictures with it, write your name in it or even print with the entire ball. If you do write

words, remember to draw the reverse image.

Stick the string down on the board either by coating one side with glue or coating the whole board with glue and rolling the string on to it and pressing it down. When the glue is dry, roll out some ink using a sheet of glass and a roller and ink up the surface of the string. Make a print on to the fabric by pushing and rubbing on the back of the board.

GLUE-PRINTING

For this technique, glue is used to draw the design on a thick piece of card or hardboard. PVA glue works well. You can also coat the card all over with glue and comb or scratch a pattern into it. Squeeze the glue from the bottle or tube and draw or write with it on the card, wait for it to dry and then roll it up with ink and print.

ROLLER-PRINTING

You can print directly on the fabric with a paint-covered roller. Rubber, sponge and lambswool rollers will create different textures, and rollers can also be cut into with a craft knife to make patterns. Either paint the paints on to the roller

String and glue prints

Prints made with rollers and brushes

with a brush (in which case you will not get a smooth print), or roll the paint out on a glass sheet (this will give you smooth bands of colour).

The quantity of paint on your roller and the pressure you apply will affect the end result. Sponge rollers can produce particularly attractive prints. If you are using long lengths of fabric, a large sponge or lambswool roller will cover your fabric with colour and texture very quickly.

BRUSH-PRINTING

You can create a vast selection of textures by printing with a variety of brushes. Dip the brush into the paint and blob off the excess, then push it gently down on to the fabric. Flat, fan, wedge, round, pointed and divided brushes will all produce different results. You can also try twisting, turning and dragging the brush for a series of different textures.

CARD-PRINTING

Card can be used for printing: the edges of boxes, corrugated card, corners and so on are all suitable. Block-card prints made from pieces of card cut and mounted on a larger piece of card are very effective. The cut

80

shapes are stuck down with gaps between them.

Roll up the block in colour using a roller and a sheet of glass, or paint directly on to the block. Print the block on to the fabric by pressing it on to the fabric firmly. You could roll over the block with clean water. If you find placing the block on to the fabric difficult, make a handle out of card and attach it to the back of the block.

RUBBER-STAMP PRINTING

Rubber stamps are very popular, and you can now buy many different ready-made rubber-stamp pictures, along with fabric-ink pads to print your stamps. Try making your own rubber stamp with an eraser. Cut areas away using a sharp knife, ink up the stamp and print.

There is also a rubber-stamp material available with which you can create your own rubber stamps. It is very flexible, easy to cut with a knife or scissors and produces very clear images. It has a peel-off paper backing, and you simply cut out your design and stick the rubber material on to some thick card or wood. Roll up with ink and print.

POLYSTYRENE PRINTING

Thin polystyrene or the thicker, more textured, tiles can be drawn on with a biro to make indentations. The polystyrene can then be rolled up with fabric paints and printed. The results are quite naïve but fairly effective.

WOOD-BLOCK PRINTING

You can buy wooden blocks for printing, or be very ambitious and carve your own using wood-cutting tools. As with all the block methods, you must make your image in reverse. Roll the ink on to the block with a roller, or paint it on direct with a brush. Be careful, as, if you use too much paint, you will create ridges of paint along the edges of the block when printing. It takes longer to paint the colour on by hand, but you can then use several colours if you wish.

LINO-PRINTING

A lino-print is made by cutting away the top surface of the lino using cutting tools. You gouge out the areas which you do not wish to print. The surface is then covered in paint using a roller, which leaves the cut areas without paint. A print can then be taken. The surface of the lino is waterproof and does not accept fabric paint too readily, but block- or lino-printing colour can be used. When printing on fabric, the lino-block can be flocked (coated in a kind of felt to help printing), but we have succeeded in printing small lengths of some thin fabrics without doing this.

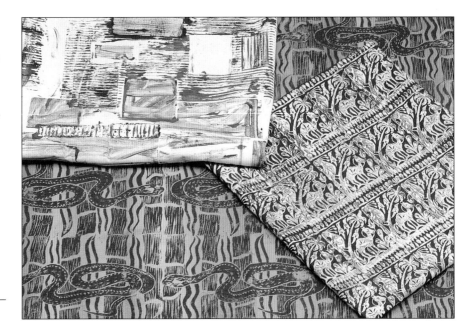

Card, wood-block and lino prints

Heating the lino gently first will make cutting into it easier. The best tools are wood-cutting tools, or special pen-type lino-cutting tools can be bought from art and craft shops. You can draw on the lino first with a felt-tip marker pen or with carbon paper and a biro before you begin to cut. Always keep your hands behind the tool so that, if you slip, there will not be a nasty accident. You can make a wooden board with a lip of wood at one end to attach to the

edge of your table to prevent slips.

As with all the blocks, you can roll the lino up with one or more colours, and you can also make two or three different blocks to print on top of one another.

TRANSFER-PRINTING

This method of printing enables you to produce quite complex designs with many colours. First the design is painted on to paper using special transfer paints, and it is then transferred to fabric by ironing with a hot iron. You can either use a lining paper, or you can buy special

transfer paper. Do not use paper that is too thick. The design that you have painted on the paper will be reproduced on the fabric. Remember to use synthetic fabric if you want bright colours.

You will find that the colours in the bottle are completely different when applied to paper than when they are transferred to fabric. Make a test chart so that you can determine what the final colours will be. All the colours are inter-mixable and can be diluted with water. They are transparent, so if you print one colour on top of another, it will result in a third colour.

Cutting lino with lino-cutting tools

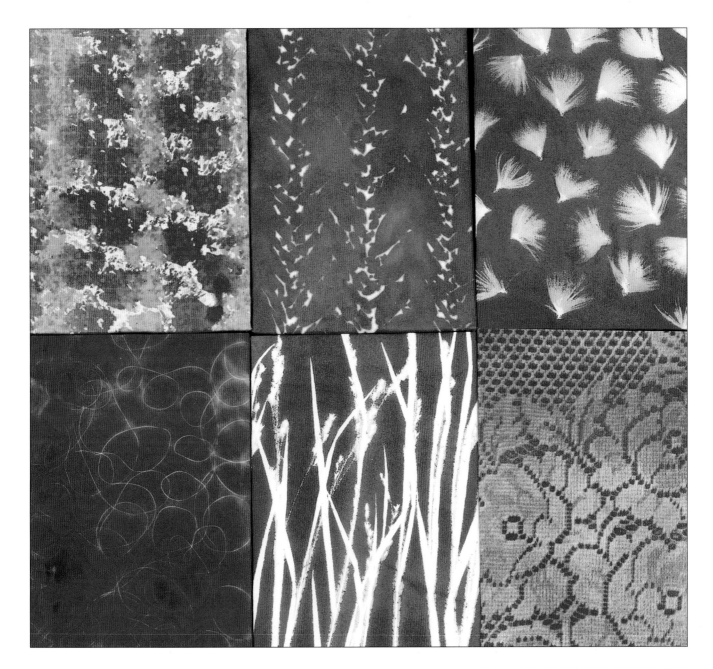

Paint your design on the paper using as many colours as you wish, and wait until it is dry before ironing. The painted paper will last a long time if you keep it in a cool, dry place, so you do not have to transfer on the same day.

The ironing part is very important. A non-steam iron – the type with no pattern or holes on the base – works best, but you can use a steam iron as long as you use it dry. The iron needs to be really hot. It must not touch the fabric, so make sure that you have another layer of paper between the fabric and the iron. Keep moving the iron slowly around; if you leave it in

Transfer prints.
(*Top row, from left to right*)
   Sponge
   Paintbrush
   Feathers
(*Bottom row, from left to right*)
   String
   Grass
   Lace

one position for too long, the shape of the iron and pattern on the underside will show on the fabric. You can peep underneath the paper to check whether the pattern is being evenly transferred. You can take two or three prints, but they will of course become paler and paler.

Try placing flat items such as feathers, string, lace, grasses or cut shapes on the transfer paper. You could also try sponging or printing on the paper and then transferring it on to the fabric.

(*Left*)
Ironing a transfer print on to fabric

Mono-print samples created with sticks, stones, fingers, combs and plants

MONO-PRINTING

A mono-print is taken by painting a design on to a sheet of glass or plastic and, while the paint is still damp, placing the fabric on the glass to take a print. Unlike block-printing, which can be repeated, mono-printing will give you only one print, so it will be unique. You can take a second print, but it will be paler than the first, so no two mono-prints can be identical.

First paint your design or picture on to the glass, or coat the glass with paint all over using a sponge, brushes or a roller. Using a stick or the wrong end of a pencil, draw outlines into the wet paint. You can also use your fingers or nails to draw a design, or create textures with combs and sponges. Try laying some pressed grasses, flowers or cut- or torn-paper shapes on to the wet paint before you take the print.

You must work fairly quickly, as the paint cannot be allowed to dry. Placing the fabric on to the glass is not easy, especially if it is a large piece. Enlist a helper and, holding each corner, let the middle down on to the glass first. Alternatively, you can stretch the fabric on to a frame and lower this gently over the sheet of glass.

SCREEN-PRINTING

Screen-printing is also known as silk-screen printing and serigraphy. It is extremely versatile and its scope for

Combing paint on a sheet of glass to use for a mono-print

creative possibilities is endless. Screen-printing is a process which uses a stencil. This is attached to a mesh fabric which has been stretched tightly over a frame. You will need paper, screen filler, wax, drawing fluid, PVA glue and shellac or profilm to make a stencil. The frame needs to be taped over at the sides and corners to prevent dye from escaping under the frame.

Screen-print samples.
(*From left to right*)
  Leaf print
  Wax print
  Cut-paper print
  Torn-paper print
  Heart shapes
  Multi-coloured butterfly print

The printing ink is drawn over the screen with a squeegee (a rubber strip attached to a length of wood), and the ink passes through the stencil on to the fabric. Nowadays there is a great selection of water-soluble textile inks, so it is easy to wash the screen and clean up. The printed fabric must be heat-set with a hot iron to make the colours permanent.

The following methods can be used to make the stencil.

Paper stencils

Simply cut or tear your design from paper and place it under the screen. This works very well with large, flat areas of colour. The stencil adheres to the screen after one pull of the squeegee and ink. You can also place leaves, flowers, grasses and pre-cut shapes under the screen.

Painted stencils

Here you can draw the design you require on to the mesh screen itself. Then paint the areas you do *not* wish to print with screen-filler, shellac, wax or PVA glue. With this method, thick and thin lines, and rough and smooth textures can be obtained.

Screen-drawing fluid can also be applied to the areas that you *do* wish to print, and then allowed to dry. Screen-filler is then coated over the entire screen using a squeegee. When this has dried, wash the areas which are to be printed with cold water. With this method, detailed linear design can be achieved.

Cut-profilm stencils

Cut the thin film with a sharp knife. Peel off the paper

backing, and melt the profilm on to the screen by ironing. The designs can be as complicated as you are able to cut. Profilm is available by the metre (or yard) from art and graphics shops.

Photo stencils

Using a special photo-emulsion mix, coat the screen using a squeegee. When dry, expose the screen to light through a positive image of the design. Letraset or ink drawings on acetate can be used. The areas not exposed to light will wash out with warm water.

You can use photographic images on the screen. There are specialist studios which can transfer your image on to the screen.

Now that you have made up your screen and stencil, it is time to start printing. Place the screen on your fabric and pour some ink along one end of the screen. Using a squeegee, push the ink through the screen on to the fabric. Remove the screen and, if you are making a repeat pattern or a number of prints, continue the process. Clean your screen immediately when you have finished printing, or the mesh will clog with dry paint.

There is a great deal of additional information available on screen-printing, for which we do not have room in this book. There are some excellent books on screen-printing on fabric if you would like to experiment more with this technique – look for these in art and craft shops and in specialist bookshops.

Screen-printing a clown design on to T-shirts

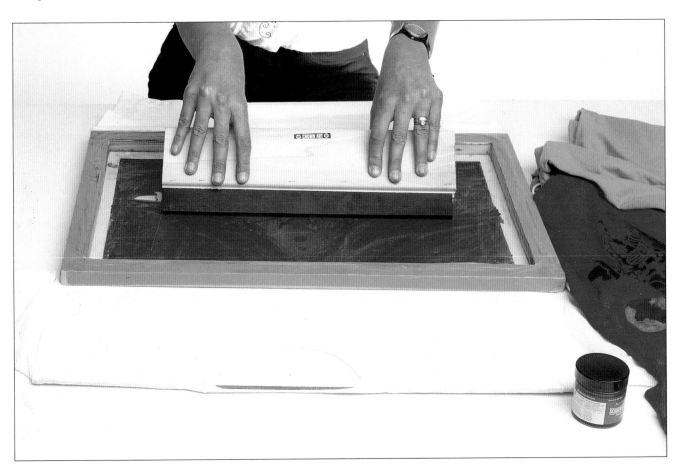

IMAGE-TRANSFER PRINTING

Simply photocopy your favourite photograph or picture and transfer it with a special product which glues the image to the fabric. This product, called 'image-maker', is available in art and craft shops.

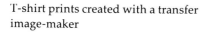

T-shirt prints created with a transfer image-maker

Equipment needed

- Image-maker liquid
- Pre-washed fabrics, e.g., T-shirts or sweatshirts
- Sponge
- Card
- Brush
- Photocopies of images to be printed

Fabrics

The results are much clearer on light-coloured fabrics. You could always paint a white area on a dark background using fabric paint, and then use the transfer on that area. Remember to fix the paints before applying the liquid. Wash any fabric prior to printing to remove any size.

Choosing your subject

All the images to be transferred must be photocopies in either black and white or colour. Remember that your photocopies will be reversed when printed, so try to use those without lettering or numbers.

Method of printing

1. Place a plastic bag or metal foil between the layers of a T-shirt or underneath a single layer of fabric.

2. Place the photocopy on a piece of foil, printed-side up, and, using a large brush, cover the surface with a layer of image-maker liquid.

3. Lift up the image and place it face-side down in the correct position on your fabric. Place a paper towel over the top and press down firmly, using a rolling pin to make sure that it is attached. Remove the paper towel.

4. Leave to dry for at least four hours.

5. Using a wet sponge, thoroughly soak the surface of the photocopy. Wait for it to soften, then peel back the top layer towards the centre of the picture. Remove the top layer completely with the sponge. Leave it to dry.

6. Remove all the 'fuzz' in further sessions of damping down and rubbing off until all the paper is removed and the image is clear.

7. When dry, seal the photocopy with a few drops of image-maker rubbed on with a brush.

Assorted ties and bow-ties created using printing techniques.
(*From left to right*)
  Ties: hand-print, rubber-stamp print with glitter pen, chamois-leather print, rag-rolling, wood-block print
(*From left to right*)
  Bow-ties: mono-print, string print, screen-print

8. Allow it to dry finally overnight. Leave for seventy-two hours before washing in lukewarm water.

9. Add extra textures to your image by applying puffa pens or outliners and glitter pens.

FINISHES

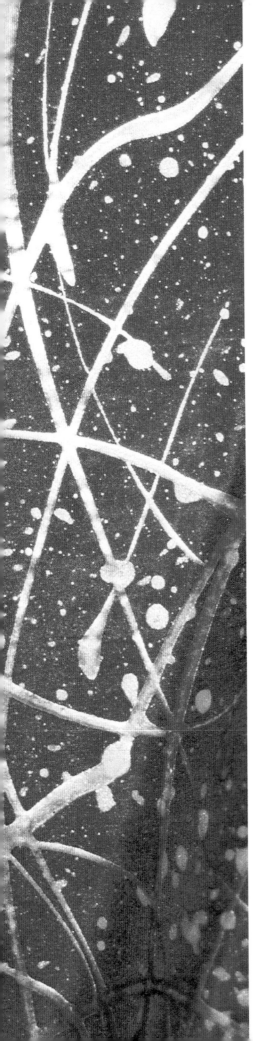

The finishes in this chapter are all easy to do. They look the same as some of the decorative paint finishes that you may have seen on walls and furniture. Now you can try some of these techniques on your furnishings too. If you cannot find just the right fabric for your curtains or cushions to match your sofa, paint your own!

Painting with sponges, sticks, rags and combs will enable you to produce textures that would be almost impossible to achieve with a brush. These textures can also be very useful as backgrounds to other techniques. They are quick and easy ways of colouring fabric and can be used to produce soft, mottled effects or a bold, dynamic look.

Equipment needed

- Fabric
- Padded surface or frame
- Masking tape
- Paints
- Saucers
- Combs, brushes, rags, sticks
- Newspaper, plastic sheeting

Fabric coloured by dribbling and flicking dyes across the surface

Fabrics

These techniques are suitable for all fabrics. Use anti-spread on silk if you find that the textures are not definite enough.

Dyes and paints

Fabric paints – both opaque and metallic – work well. Transparent paints can be used on light-coloured fabrics. If you are using more than one colour, remember that additional colours will be created where they overlap. Dyes also work, but are too thin for some techniques, although they can be thickened. Diluted gutta can also be used. Bronze powders and pearl-lustre pigments can be mixed with the paints. A special spatter paint is available, and is sold in a bottle with a pump action. Prepare all your colours before you begin, using one dish or saucer for each colour.

Sponges, combs, and other tools

Invest in a natural sponge if you can, as these are softer to work with and their non-uniform shapes produce more interesting textures than some of the synthetic varieties. You can buy pre-cut sponge shapes or cut your own from big car or bath sponges.

Collect some combs – the wide-toothed types work well – or make your own comb with stiff card. DIY shops and cake

Equipment used for finishes. Metallic paints and guttas were used in the samples.
(*Left*)
 Sponged
(*Centre, top*)
 Combed
(*Centre, bottom*)
 Flicked
(*Right*)
 Rag-rolled

decorators also have some wonderful plastic tools for plastering and icing! Specialist paint-finishing suppliers sell all sorts of tools too. You will need bristle brushes, nailbrushes, toothbrushes, cotton rags and sticks. Special stippling brushes are expensive, as they are made of badger hair.

Preparation

Before you start, cover all nearby surfaces, carpets and walls with newspaper or plastic sheeting. These are extremely messy techniques. You could always wait for a nice day and work outside.

Stretch the fabric on to a padded, flat surface with masking tape. Alternatively, some of the techniques, such as flicking, dribbling and spattering, can be carried out with the fabric stretched across a frame. Pin the fabric on to the frame, wrong-side up, and then turn the frame over on to the padded surface. If you do this, the fabric will be nice and taut but the edges will remain

unpainted. Line up your various tools and paints in saucers ready to start.

SPONGING

Sponging is very easy. Simply dab the sponge into the saucer of paint, test on scrap paper to remove excess paint, and then, using light dabs, sponge on to the fabric. The only problem is knowing when to stop. Long lengths of fabric can be covered evenly and quickly, and this method uses little paint so it is very economical.

Try to sponge evenly all over the fabric, but randomly, not in uniform rows. If you are using more than one colour, make sure that the first colour is dry before applying more colour, unless you want a softer look. You can also sponge on to a wet background for an impressionist look. Try leaving gaps between the dabs and actually letting the shape of the sponge show in the finished design.

The different textures obtained will depend entirely on the type of fabric; whether the fabric is wet, damp or dry; the texture of the sponge; how much paint you let the sponge soak up; and how hard you press with the sponge on to the surface of the fabric. If you have been a little heavy-handed, press a clean sponge on to the wet fabric paint and lift off some of the colour. If one colour looks too dominant, sponge over again with one of the other colours. Wait for the fabric to dry before removing it to fix.

RAG-ROLLING

Rag-rolling is also very easy and, like sponging, it can be carried out in one, two or more colours. It can be done with old cotton rags, or you can also try using paper towels, plastic bags, fabrics with texture such as corduroy, and even clingfilm.

Use dry rags and do not roll them but crumple or scrunch them. It is the folds and creases which make the pattern when the crumpled rag is rolled across the fabric. Dip the crumpled rag into the saucer of paint and remove excess by wiping on a piece of paper, then roll the rag along the fabric. Try to achieve an even coating randomly across the fabric; if the rag gets too clogged with paint, use a new one. Wait for the fabric to dry before fixing.

Sponging on to a pre-painted background

Rag-rolling on to a pre-painted background

COMBING

Combing can be very effective, and many different patterns and textures can be created. Curves, swirls, checks, basketweave, zig-zags, arches, spirals and linear patterns can be made by pulling the paint-laden comb in different directions across the fabric.

Wonderful combing patterns can be easily obtained using a mono-print (see page 85). Here, however, rather than scratching

Combing with a de-icer scraper

off the paint with a comb as you would do on plaster or wood, you can actually comb on the paint quite successfully. You can also coat the fabric in a thin layer of screen-printing ink with plenty of extender or diluted gutta, and then comb the paint off. You can finger-paint on this and create a design using your fingers and nails! Combing leaves the fabric quite stiff and, if too much paint is used, ridges of paint will occur all along the edges of the comb lines.

This technique of combing will only work when the fabric paints can sit on the surface of the fabric. Try leather or suede, or coat a layer of anti-spread on to silk and use thickened silk dyes. This can be an expensive method, however, and it may actually be simpler to take a mono-print.

STIPPLING

This is a very delicate finish and is not quite as easy as it looks. A bristle brush is dipped in paint and dabbed on to fabric so that the end of each bristle leaves a tiny dot. It is quite difficult to obtain an all-over even colour.

Small areas can be stippled with a stencil brush or nailbrush, but larger areas will require a stipple brush. Several colours, indeed as many as you like, can be used. Wait for the paint to dry between coats.

SPATTERING

This texture is built up by larger dots of colour than stippling, and has more of a random effect. Dip the brush into fairly thick paint and, holding it about 6 cm (2½ in) away from the fabric, run a wooden stick or your thumbnail across the bristles. Droplets of paint will spatter all over the fabric. For a thicker, more abstract spatter, load the stick with paint and just shake it up and down or tap it on the palm of your hand. Try spattering on wet fabric and try using very thin or very thick paint. Allow the fabric to dry before fixing.

FLICKING

This is basically the same technique as spattering. Use paint straight from the pot. Dip

Flicking and spattering with a toothbrush

a stick or the wooden end of a brush into the paint and flick it, using your wrist. Long dashes and loops of colour will cover your fabric. Keep changing directions, flicking from different angles. This may take some time to dry if you have been using thick paint. Allow the fabric to dry before fixing.

DRIBBLING

Dribble runny fabric paint or diluted gutta all over the fabric. If your fabric is stretched on to a frame or taped to a board, try standing it up so that the dribbles run down the fabric. Tilt the frame and change directions. Try the technique on wet fabric, using many colours. Allow the fabric to dry before fixing.

Try using two or three of the different finishing techniques on the same fabric. Try masking off areas of fabric with masking tape, wax or masking fluid, and texture certain areas only. Pleat, gather or crumple the fabric so that the spatters or flicks will not be evenly distributed. Experiment and try to create some of the more difficult paint finishes such as wood-graining, tortoise-shelling and faux marbling. Do ensure that your fabric is dry before you untape it, or it may smudge. Fix the paints using the method suited to those used (see pages 120–3).

Richly trimmed cushions using the various decorative finishes

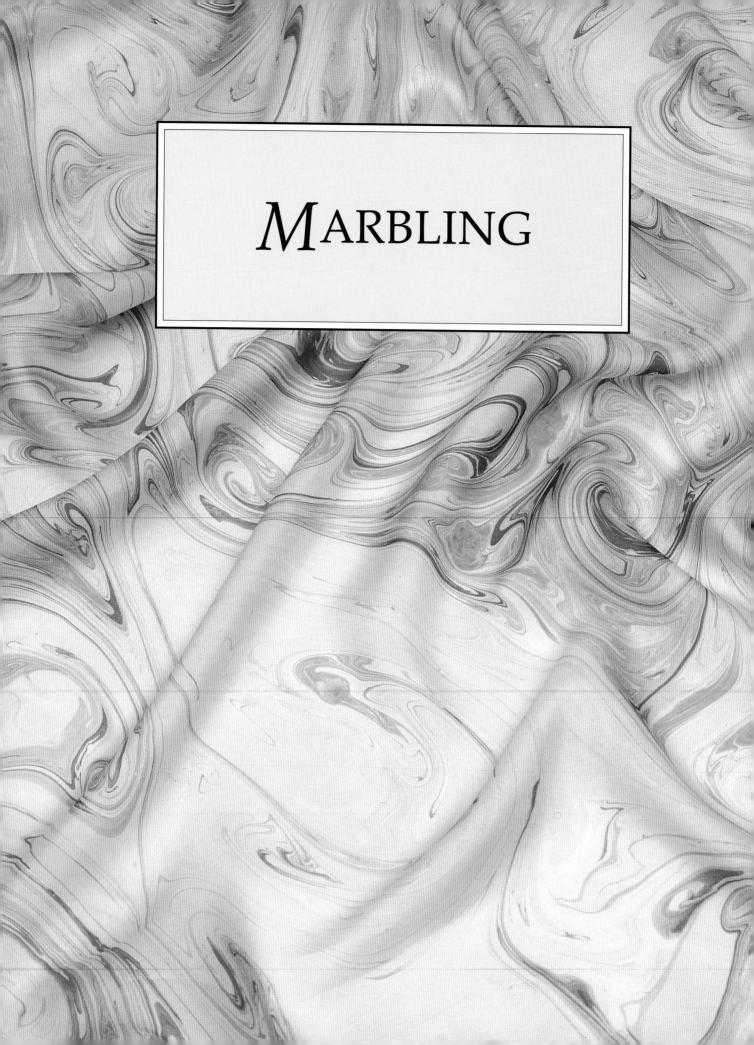

MARBLING

Marbling on fabric is great fun, and is a wonderful technique with which to experiment. Each design created is unique and can never be repeated. You simply float the fabric paints on a prepared medium or size, and then mix and swirl your fabric colours with various tools, brushes and combs into fascinating patterns. The fabric is then laid down on top of the size and the paint sticks to the fabric so that the pattern is transferred to it. A new and unique pattern is created each time a transfer or pick-up is made. The fabric is then rinsed with cold water and fixed with a hot iron.

Equipment needed

- Fabric and alum
- Frame or tray
- Medium: carrageenan, tragacanth gum, wallpaper paste, liquid starch, Irish moss tea, gelatine or ready-to-mix marbling medium
- Paints and oxgall
- Applicators
- Tools for pattern-making
- Newspaper strips

Blue-and-yellow freestyle technique on silk

Marbling frame

While you are experimenting with small pieces of fabric, you can use a deep dish or tray. Pet-litter trays or developing trays from photographic studios are ideal; you can even use your roasting-tin. It does make it easier if you use a transparent or white container, as you are then able to see the fabric paints floating on the size.

If you are really keen to embark on a large project, perhaps some 90 × 90 cm (36 × 36 in) silk scarves, it may be a good idea to build your own frame. A square or rectangle of wood which can hold a heavy plastic liner is all that you need. You could attach a base to the wooden frame, but this will make it very heavy, so you could just use a table instead. The frame can be fixed with metal angles and lined with clear plastic. Make sure that the plastic is folded neatly in the corners with no escape route for the liquid.

Medium

The consistency of the medium (size or base) is absolutely crucial to the success of this technique. There are several thickening agents which can be used to prepare the medium – we have found the carrageenan to be the best. When preparing the medium use distilled water, as hard water will not make a good medium. Keep the size at room temperature.

99

Carrageenan

This is a seaweed, used as an emulsifier in food. It can be bought in some art shops or by mail order, and comes in granules, chips or powder form. The blender variety, which requires no cooking, is the most convenient. First mix 75 g (3 oz) of carrageenan with 575 ml (one pint) of warm water in a blender. Add this to 3·5 litres

(*Left*)
Equipment needed for marbling

Black, pink and turquoise marbling

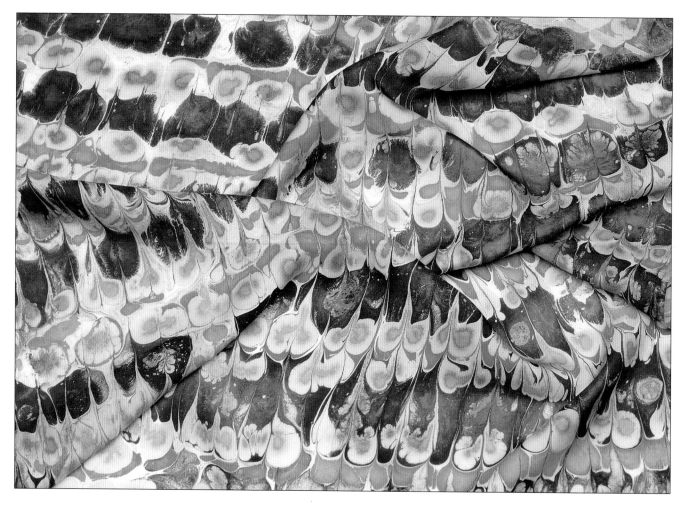

(six pints) of distilled water and stir. Keep repeating this until you have enough to fill your tray or frame up to 4 cm (1½ in) in depth. Leave the medium for at least twelve hours and keep the surface as clean as possible.

Tragacanth gum

This is a gum plant, also used as an emulsifier in food. It can be purchased by mail order (not many art shops stock it). Mix 15 ml (one tablespoon) of gum tragacanth with 1·2 litres (two pints) of hot distilled water (a blender can be used for this). Leave it for twenty-four hours and then stir in another 1·2 litres (two pints) of water just before you are ready to marble.

Wallpaper paste

This can of course be bought at your local DIY shop. Mix as the instructions dictate and try to achieve the consistency of double cream. You can marble with this medium after thirty minutes.

Liquid starch

This can be bought in the supermarket and used undiluted. Starch can also be bought in powder form and mixed to a thick solution.

Irish moss tea

This is available from health-food stores. Mix 25 g (1 oz) of ground Irish moss to 2·3 litres (four pints) of boiling water. Cook this for five minutes and then add 575 ml (one pint) of cold water.

Gelatine

This can be purchased from the supermarket and mixed with hot water. Follow the instructions on the packet and aim for the consistency of heavy cream.

Marbling medium

Craft shops sell packets of ready-to-mix medium especially for marbling.

Starch, wallpaper paste and tragacanth gum can keep for long periods, whereas carrageenan starts to go mouldy after four to five days at room temperature. The medium can be re-used; store it in the fridge and then make sure you bring it up to room temperature before using again. To keep the medium clean between designs, skim the surface with strips of newspaper.

Fabrics

Any fabric – natural or synthetic – can be marbled. We find that fine cottons, polyesters and silks work best. The more finely woven the fabric, the more effectively the pattern is picked up. Heavily-textured fabrics such as velvet, towelling and wild silk are not a good idea.

Preparing the fabric

Always wash and thoroughly rinse the fabric to remove any size. Better results will be obtained if you coat the fabric evenly with alum before marbling, as this makes the fabric very receptive to the paints. Add 30 ml (two tablespoons) of alum to 1·2 litres (two pints) of warm water and stir until dissolved. This solution will keep for a week.

Dip the fabric into the solution, making sure that it is completely coated. If the alum is mixed too strongly or left on too long, the fabric will rot and actually disintegrate. Let the fabric drip-dry; do not put it in a tumble-drier as this produces static electricity which makes it very difficult to lay the fabric on the medium. When dry and coated with alum, the fabric will feel a little stiff. Press it with a medium-heat iron, as wrinkles or creases in the fabric will spoil the pattern.

Paints

The paints must be able to float on the medium. All is not lost if they sink as soon as you apply them, however, as they can be thinned with oxgall. Paints to use include fabric paints, acrylics, oil-based paints and fabric dyes. The oil-based paints and some acrylics can only be used on fabrics which will not be washed. Specialized paints for marbling can also be bought in craft shops.

Always test the medium and paints to check that you have the correct consistencies. If the paints are too thick, they will sink to the bottom, and if they are too thin, they will disperse too quickly until they are almost invisible.

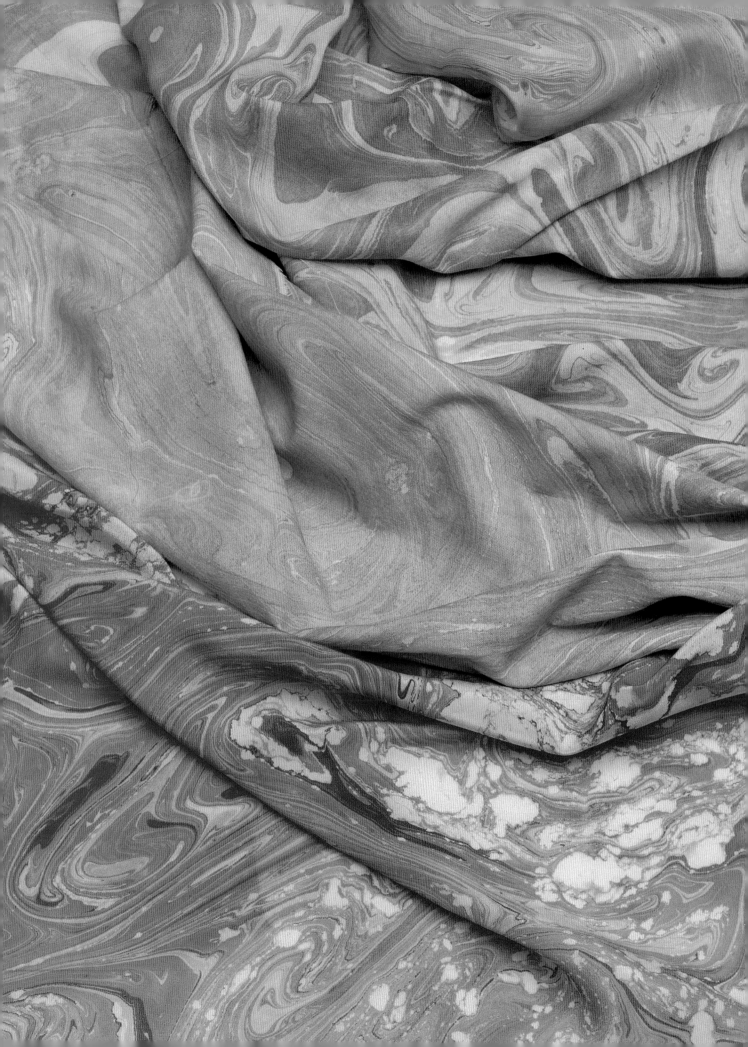

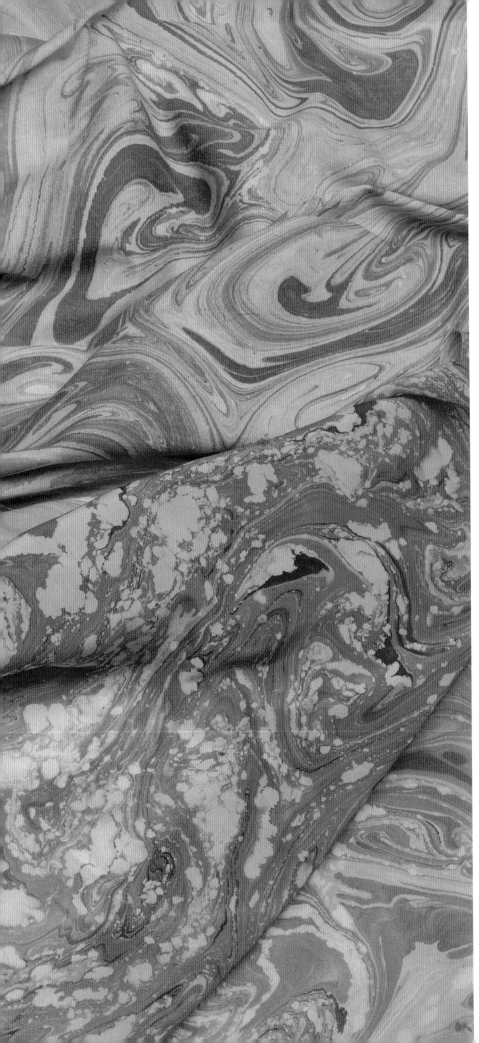

(*Above*)
Dropping dyes on to a marbling base of carrageenan in a large frame

(*Left*)
Vibrant pinks and blues on cotton fabrics

Applicators

You will need an assortment of applicators for applying the paints to the medium. Small eye-droppers, large medicine syringes, toothbrushes, spray bottles and atomizers are all useful. Another good tool is a whisk made of bristles from a kitchen broom, gathered up and fixed at one end with tape.

Tools for pattern-making

Another set of tools will be required to create the patterns in the paints on the medium. Collect together an assortment of items such as combs, toothpicks, feathers and knitting needles. Make a comb as wide as your frame with a piece of wood and nails. We made a very successful comb with golf tees!

103

FLOATING PAINTS AND MAKING PATTERNS

Start by skimming the surface of the size with newspaper strips to remove any dirt, grease and dust, and then very gently float the paints on the surface of the medium. Each drop of paint, if it is of the correct consistency, will spread to a 5–8 cm (2–3 in) circle. Some paint may sink, especially if you drop it heavily from a height. Don't worry about this, as long as most of the paint floats on the surface. The more colours you add to the size, the more intense the colours become, as they do not mix but squeeze in next to each other.

If your paints won't spread, colour unevenly or have ragged edges, it may be that your size is too thick, in which case you can add more distilled water. It may be that the size is too hot or too cold – it needs to be at room temperature. If the paints spread too far, they are too thin. If they sink, they may need another drop of oxgall.

Now the fun part begins. Use your collection of tools to create swirls, blobs and other patterns. You can create various definite patterns, as well as a range of wonderful freestyle designs.

Dramatic effects in marbled pictures

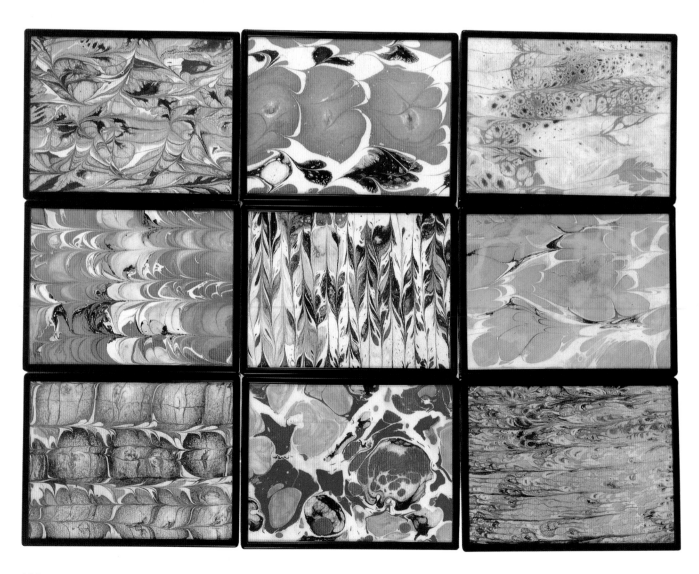

Stones

Drop drops of colour – both small and large – next to each other. No combing or swirling is needed here.

Spirals

Drop colours in rows of circles and then draw spirals with a toothpick in each circle.

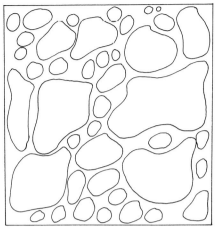

Stones

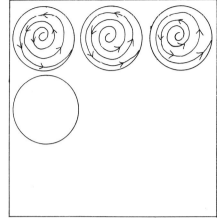

Spirals

Hearts

Drop circles of colour all over the size and then pull a toothpick down the middle of each circle in one direction only.

Flowers

Drop circles of colour at random or in rows and then draw with the toothpick four or five times from the outer edge to the middle of the circle.

Hearts

Flowers

Veins

Spray or drop many small droplets all over the fabric, then spray or use the whisk with some oxgall. This will disperse the paints, leaving small thin veins.

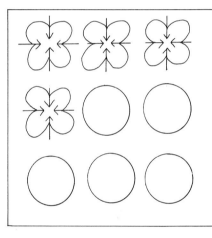

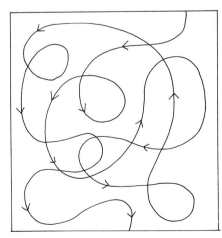

Freestyle

This is easy. Just swirl the paint all over in different directions with a toothpick or comb.

Veins

Freestyle

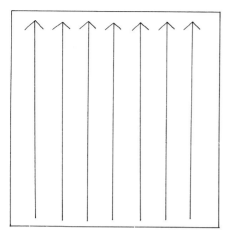

Arches

Feathering

Arches

(a) Use a comb and keep the pulls in one direction.
(b) For more definite arches, pull the comb across the fabric at right angles to the first combing. This will look like an Austrian blind.

These designs can look very different, depending on how far apart the teeth are spaced in your comb.

Feathering

(a) Trail the comb one way and then back the other way between the first set of lines.
(b) Repeat the same operation, but at right angles to the first set of combing, for a finer look.

Do have fun and experiment. You can try all sorts of exciting ideas. Try combining some of the methods: for instance, after creating the feather design, add some small droplets or paint; or try combing wavy or zig-zag lines on top of a straight set of lines.

PICKING UP
THE PATTERN

Picking up or transferring the pattern you have designed from the medium to the fabric is really exciting. Lay the fabric down on the surface and leave it for about five seconds, or until you can see that the colour has soaked through, and then lift it off. If you find the fabric too difficult to control, stretch it over a frame first, and then gently lower this on to the medium.

When marbling a large piece of fabric, try to enlist a helper, as it is so much easier when there are two of you to lay down and lift off the fabric. Let the middle touch the surface of the medium first, then very gently roll down the ends. Try not to trap air underneath or air bubbles will form and make plain areas on the fabric. When lifting the fabric off, let the excess medium drip back into the frame.

If the paints are not being picked up by the fabric or the design is streaky or patchy, the fabric may not have received an even coating of alum. Plain patches will occur where air bubbles are left in the medium, or if the fabric has not been ironed flat.

After picking up the fabric, rinse it gently with clean water or hang it on the washing line and use the sprinkler on the hose. Try not to touch the pattern while rinsing as it is easily smeared until it is dry. Let the marbled fabric rest for a couple of days before ironing on the reverse side to heat-fix the paints. You may gently hand-wash or dry-clean marbled fabrics.

There are many variables in this technique, and it is difficult for a complete novice to get everything perfect the first time. After practice, however, you will

be able to try all sorts of exciting ideas. Try moving the fabric in small jerks as you lay it on to the medium; this creates little steps. Areas of the fabric can be coated with masking fluid, wax, gutta or masking tape before it is laid down on the medium. You could try over-marbling, or shadow marbling, as it is also called. When the first pattern is dry, pick up another pattern on the same piece of fabric to create exciting effects.

A desk set, folders and boxes beautifully decorated with marbled fabrics

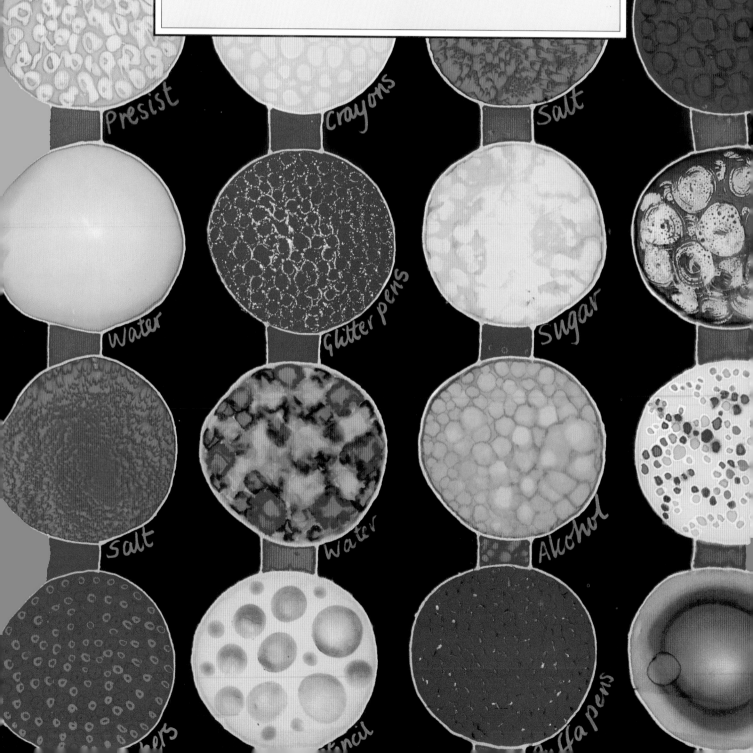

COMBINED
TECHNIQUES

wax

Presist

crayons

Salt

Water

Glitter pens

Sugar

Salt

Water

Alcohol

ers

Stencil

uffa pens

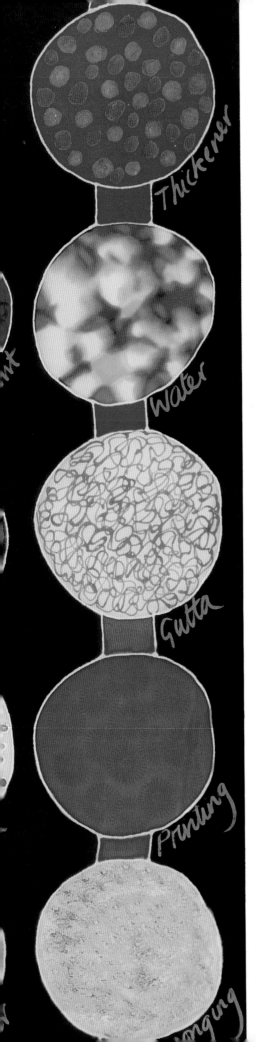

Now that you have read about all the various techniques, you will be able to try two, three or even more of these on one design. By experimenting you will learn which techniques complement each other, and, by using these together, you can achieve quite complex designs.

It can be very effective to paint your fabric first using, for example, a watercolour, spray or sponging technique. Next, paint on top of this, either directly on to the fabric or using another technique such as one of the resists, stencilling or printing. You could try marbling the background and then covering areas of the marbling with wax before applying a dye. A similar idea could be carried out with a tie-dye, batik or sprayed background.

The possibilities are endless, and once you start combining techniques, ideas will come flooding to you. You will find yourself thinking, 'What if I used transfer paints and took a mono-print, and then used a resist on top of this and finished with some hand-painting, using some metallic powders mixed in the paint?' Or, 'Perhaps if I spattered a watercolour background in three colours, I could screen-print over that and put some final intricate details on with a puffa pen'!

Before you get carried away, however, there are certain factors of which you will need to be aware when combining techniques. If you have used a resist technique, for example, you will need to remove the resist and fix the dyes before applying puffa pens. If you have used anti-spread, gutta may not work properly on this as it does not penetrate the fabric, so use a tjanting or wax brush instead.

When applying many coats of dye, be careful if you are using water-based gutta or wax substitute. The barrier can be weakened by the solvents and water in the dyes, and so you may have to re-apply your resist. If you have used water-based gutta, sugar syrup or wax substitute, you obviously cannot soak the fabric in a dyebath as they will begin to dissolve.

When many coats of dye are applied to thin fabrics, the dark pigments move towards the resist lines and create a dark edge. This is actually very effective, but, if it is not wanted, you must fix the dyes into the fabric before applying another coat of dye. Remember when fixing that some guttas and wax especially may not continue to act as resists when they have been in the steamer.

This amazing sample shows how you can combine many of the different techniques on one piece of work. Careful planning may be needed, but it is possible

Water-based guttas and wax substitute can leave a pale outline when removed (see the Cock-a-doodle-doo fabric shown here). If you do not want this, use wax or a solvent-based gutta.

If you are painting on thicker fabrics you can simply over-paint, starting of course with the paler colours. If you need to paint very long lengths of fabric, think about painting or stencilling techniques on spattered, sponged or rag-rolled backgrounds, which are fairly quick to do.

Permanent markers, dyes and glitter pens can be useful for adding the details needed to complete a design, as in the Sarah's farm design shown here. This was hand-painted on a mono-print background.

Three very different pieces.
(*From left to right*)
   Cock-a-doodle-doo: watercolour, gutta and salt
   Sarah's farm: mono-print, painting direct and puffa pens
   New Forest: wax, sponging and painting direct

A beautiful patchwork quilt and cushions, hand-pieced and quilted. The brightly patterned fabric pieces were painted using the sun technique (see page 20)

You can of course enhance your designs further with needlework techniques such as embroidery, beading, quilting, patchwork and appliqué. You can even tear the fabric into strips and weave it. Patchwork and appliqué can be seen in the photograph above. Beading and embroidery are shown on the tie-dye wallhanging on pages 4–5.

It is easier to cover up mistakes when you use two or three techniques. You can cover splodges with a sponged or salted background. Use a marker or puffa pen to cover marks, or

incorporate the mark into a hand-painted motif. You could appliqué something over the mistake or use embroidery and beading to cover it up.

If a piece of work really cannot be redeemed, use good areas of the fabric to make cards or brooches, or to cover a book or small box. If you are in extremity, do not despair! Tear your mistake into smaller pieces to be used for appliqué and patchwork.

Combining some of the many fabric-painting techniques will enable you to achieve any design you like – just think the whole process through from beginning to end. Will it need fixing halfway through? Will the resist need removing before you continue? If you dry-clean or wash the fabric, will the paints, crayons or pens melt or disappear?

You will probably make a few mistakes along the way, but you

Underwater dolphins make a lively design on this beautiful aqua-coloured scarf

will soon learn what works, what to avoid and which fabrics to use. We hope, whatever you do, that you have found this book helpful, and, above all, that you enjoy your work and take pleasure in its results for years to come.

113

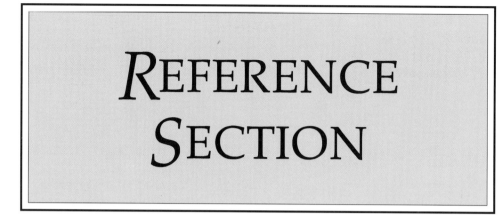

REFERENCE SECTION

FABRICS

Before you embark on the exciting painting on of colour, consider the fabrics to be used: their fibre, feel, cost, quality and effect are extremely important. The final piece of work will only suit its purpose if the correct technique is applied to the correct fabric at the outset.

Fibres fall into two main categories: man-made and natural. Man-made fabrics are now produced with a more 'natural' feel and quality, and blends of natural and man-made fibres are readily available. This can be a problem for fabric painters, as many of the dyes and paints produced can be used on either natural *or* man-made fabrics, not both.

Buying fabric direct from fabric- or silk-painting suppliers is a sensible idea, as they will cater specifically for your needs. You will be looking mainly for light-coloured fabrics: white or natural off-white and cream. It may be useful to find a fabric with a background colour to suit your piece of work, rather than having to paint it first. Check that the colours you require will over-print well on to a coloured background. Sometimes a stripe or check can be over-printed with an interesting effect. Remember that all your fabrics should be washed or dry-cleaned before use to remove finish added during the manufacturing process (see page 124). Finish may sometimes be used to advantage as a resist, but normally this is not the case.

Fabric samples.
(*Clockwise from left*)
   Silk
   Man-made fabrics
   Nylon
   Cotton
   Wool

Cotton

Cotton is a natural fibre, and is very strong both when wet and dry. It is absorbent, dyes easily and can be bleached. Cotton can be washed at high temperatures, but creases badly.

Fabric names

Butter muslin, calico, canvas, challis, cheesecloth, chintz, corduroy, denim, gabardine, lace, organdie, poplin, sailcloth, scrim, sheeting, towelling, velvet.

Silk

Silk is a natural fibre which drapes beautifully and is soft to handle and wear. It is lustrous, and dyes well with vibrant colours. Silk is absorbent, but is weak when wet and is also weakened by sunlight and bleach. It creases when washed and yellows with age.

Fabric names

Bourrette, brocade, chiffon, crêpe de Chine, douppion, Duchesse satin, georgette, honan, mousseline, organza, pongée (habutai, Jap silk), sandwashed satin, tussah (*soie sauvage*, wild silk), velvet.

Wool

Wool is a natural fibre. It is absorbent and dyes well, but shrinks when rubbed or washed in hot water. It is attacked by moths and sunlight. Wool drapes well and is warm to wear. It is crease-resistant.

Fabric names

Broadcloth, domette, etamine, felt, flannel, jersey, wool crêpe.

Linen

Linen is a natural fibre which is very strong but creases extensively. It is absorbent, although strong colours may bleed and the fabric can shrink, so wash at a lower temperature.

Fabric names

Crash, handkerchief linen, linen canvas.

Nylon

Nylon is a man-made fibre. It dyes with difficulty, but is useful for the transfer-printing technique. Nylon is produced in a variety of textures, from hard to soft and fine to bulky.

Polyester

Polyester is a man-made fibre, and is manufactured in many weights, textures and weaves. It can be permanently pleated.

Viscose

Viscose is a man-made fibre whose qualities resemble natural fibres. It is often added to other fabrics to create versatile blends.

Resist and permanent marker pen used on lovely, fine chiffon silk with subtle rose motif

PAINTS AND DYES

As the popularity of fabric painting has grown, many new paints and dyes have been produced. There are now so many colourants on the market that it is difficult to know which to buy for your project. They do not all work equally well on all fabrics, so do be sure to read the manufacturer's instructions on the techniques of applying the paints or dyes, and the method of fixing the colour into the fabric.

When deciding which dyes or paints to use, you will first need to know the type of fabric on which you are going to paint. Will you be using a thick canvas or calico, or a thin silk or nylon? You must also consider the technique you will be using. Will you be airbrushing or screen-printing; tie-dyeing or marbling? Have you access to a steamer? If not, use heat-set paints.

The cost of the fabric may also enter into your decision. To save time and expense, always test your technique and paints on a small sample of fabric before you begin.

The difference between dyes and paints is simply that dyes bond with the fibres and become part of the fabric, whereas paints sit on the surface of the fabric. Dyes need to be steam-fixed or fixed in a liquid fix with the use of chemicals, whereas paints can just be fixed by heat (see page 120). Air-cure dyes have recently arrived on

the market which do not need heat or steam (see page 118).

There are acid and fibre-reactive dyes, paints, silk dyes and paints, transfer paints, screen-printing inks and a large variety of pens, crayons and markers. In this book, when talking of colourants, we have used the words paints or dyes.

Fabric paints

These can be used on all fabrics, and can be mixed to create a limitless range of colours. They come in different types: opaque, transparent, fluorescent, metallic and pearlized. The opaque pale colours and metallics can be used on dark-coloured fabrics, but the transparent paints will not show up on dark fabric. The transparent paints are useful for overlapping and layering, and these are the ones to use if you are trying the sun technique (see page 20) on silk or cotton.

Some brands of fabric paints are much thicker than others, but they can be diluted easily with water or indeed thickened with Manutex. When thickened, they can be used for techniques such as screen-printing and stencilling; when thinned they can be used for the resist techniques and airbrushing. They are fixed by heat, and after fixing the colours are fast and fade-resistant.

A selection of fabric-painting materials and equipment

Fabric dyes

Fabric dyes can be used on both natural and synthetic fibres. There are hot- and cold-water dyes available, but we just use the cold (and warm) dyes and

not the hot variety. Cold-water dyes can be used to dye anything in your washing machine, although they really only work on natural fabrics. They are normally purchased in powder form. There is a vast colour range and they are very economical.

Fibre-reactive dyes are perfect for natural fabrics. They can be used in your washing machine. They can also be used to hand dye in a bucket, dip dye, vat dye or be used to paint, spray, sponge or spatter your fabric. Liquid fibre-reactive dyes are now available.

Once you have mixed the dyes, they should be used up within a couple of months, but

in powder form they will last for up to three years. They are non-toxic and the colour produced will change depending on the strength of the dye mixture, the type and quantity of fabric and the length of time you leave the fabric in the dye.

To fix some of these dyes, you will need to add chemicals, or you can buy a packet of Afterfix to paint on after painting. Some dyes need steaming or air-curing, or you can batch-set them. Be sure to read the instructions on the manufacturer's label. Not everybody wants to put the effort into mixing powders and chemicals, but the Procion colours are well worth it.

Silk dyes and paints

There is a wide range of dyes and paints on the market made especially for silk painting. They also work on wool. They can be categorized according to their method of fixing: steam- and liquid-fixed silk dyes, or heat-fixed silk paints.

Steam- and liquid-fixed silk dyes

These are transparent and penetrate the fabric thoroughly. They are wonderful to use and the depth of colour increases after fixing. These dyes contain alcohol and they are very concentrated: they need diluting up to four times with water or alcohol before use. These silk dyes can also be added to a

thickener and used for printing techniques and stencilling. They come in a wide range of colours and work beautifully with the salt, water and alcohol techniques. All manufacturers will have their own instructions when it comes to mixing, diluting and fixing.

Heat-fixed silk paints

These can be used on other fabrics as well as silk and wool. They are very popular, as they are so easy to fix quickly with the use of heat. Some leave a little stiffness in the fabric, especially if it has been coated in several layers. Silk paints do not spread as far as the dyes, and sometimes the reverse side is not as vibrant as the top side.

Some techniques, especially alcohol, are less effective with these paints. However, they are easy to use, and other heat-fixed dyes can be used with them. After fixing they are machine-washable, dry-cleanable and fade-resistant.

Dyes and paints both have their advantages, and, as you experiment, you will find a brand to suit you.

Air-cure dyes

These newly available dyes require neither steam nor heat to fix them. They bond instantly and work on silk, wool and nylon. The colours are extremely vibrant. They do not spread as easily as silk dyes and the colours react very quickly, so you will need to work fast.

You can buy a special liquid to pre-paint or spray on the fabric which improves the receptivity of the fabric to the dyes. Remember that they need no fixing: after air-curing for twenty-four hours, simply rinse to remove excess dye and iron.

Transfer paints

These are designed for use on man-made fabrics only, but we have found them useful on natural fabrics if a paler, more subdued look is required. The colours can be mixed and diluted with water, but they should not be mixed with other fabric paints or dyes.

On paper, before the transfer process is carried out, the colours look dull, but after ironing they are very, very bright. You can see on page 84 the difference between the colours on paper and the vibrant colours on polyester. After ironing for at least five minutes, they are washable and dry-cleanable.

Screen-printing inks

Screen-printing inks are very concentrated and, unless you buy them ready-mixed, they need to be mixed, a few drops at a time, with a binder. The inks are water-soluble, so screen-cleaning is easy, and they can be mixed with each other to create new colours. They are suitable for any fabric and they are fixed by heat. Fabric paints and dyes and silk dyes can be used for screen-printing when thickened

Swatches of brightly coloured fabric.
(*From left to right*)
 Top row: pastel, hot, cool
 Bottom row: bright, natural,
 psychedelic

with Manutex. Do not use air-cure dyes, as they dry too quickly and would clog the screen.

Crayons

Fabric crayons

These crayons can be used on all fabrics. There are two types of crayons: steam-fixed and iron-fixed. Crayons look the same on fabric as they do on paper. They are ideal for children to use, and after fixing they are fade-resistant and machine-washable.

Transfer crayons

These look the same as fabric crayons but, as with transfer paints, the design is drawn on to paper and then transferred on to the fabric. These crayons work on synthetic fabrics (polyester) and, like transfer paints, the colours look different on paper. The crayons are fixed by heat,

ironing on the wrong side for at least five minutes.

Stencil crayons

These crayons make stencilling very easy. They consist of oil paint in a stick and they blend and shade very easily. They are fade-resistant, but some of the crayons can only be used on non-washable fabric.

Spray paint

Cans of car-spray paint can be used, but they really do stiffen the fabric. Spray paint made especially for fabric, although hard to find, is now available. Airbrush-equipment specialists will stock spray paints and dyes, but, in fact, most paints and dyes can be diluted and used for spraying. Do not use air-cure dyes in an airbrush as they are prone to clogging. Silk paints also tend to clog the nozzle of an airbrush, but silk dyes are ideal to work with.

Felt-tip pens

Non-toxic felt-tip pens especially designed for drawing on fabric are now available. These pens are ideal for children as they are clean and easy to use. Some need fixing by heat or steam and some brands need no fixing. They are fade-resistant and machine-washable. Some types are refillable and new felt tips can be bought. Thin-tipped pens are useful for fine detailing and for making corrections.

Permanent marker pens

These can be found in all stationery shops. The thin gold and silver permanent marker pens are particularly useful for fine details and outlining. Black markers are very useful for signing your work and for delicate detailed work. Permanent marker pens need no fixing.

Puffa paint

Puffa paint or heat-expanding paint works on all fabrics. If it is used on thin fabrics such as silk or georgette, however, the fabric will pucker. It is very easy to handle as it can be used straight from the pen or applied with a brush. It expands on heating with a hairdryer.

Three-dimensional and glitter pens

These are water-based, acrylic, non-toxic and need no fixing. They can be used to add detail and dimension to your work. They can be purchased in the form of pens, bottles and tubes, and come in all colours, as well as fluorescent, glitter, pearlized and metallic. The paint remains on the surface of the fabric as a raised plastic line, so it can be used to great effect on dark fabrics.

Some outliner pens require heat setting with an iron on the back of the fabric. Iron for up to three minutes.

FIXING AND AFTERCARE

The dyes and paints need to be fixed permanently into the fabric to allow it to be washed and to prevent fading. Depending on the method of painting and the colours used, there are several methods of doing this: heating, steaming, using chemicals and air-curing. Always read the manufacturer's label to find out which method to use.

Heat-fixing

The paints which require heat for fixing can be fixed by pressing the fabric thoroughly with a hot, dry iron on the reverse side of the fabric for a few minutes. Set the temperature of the iron as recommended by the dye manufacturer. Do not use a steam iron as moisture could mark the fabric (especially silks). Protect your ironing-board with a layer of clean paper or cloth, as coloured outliners, crayons and pens can sometimes print on to it.

Place a piece of paper or cloth over polyester or other synthetic fabrics when ironing, as the synthetics cannot take the intensity of heat needed to set the dyes. If you are setting dyes on very heavy fabrics such as calico or canvas, you must iron for longer (five to six minutes).

Alternatively, you can fix awkward shapes such as lampshades and plimsolls with a hairdryer on a hot setting. This takes some time and care must be taken not to burn the item. You can also set dyes on large items in a tumble-drier, or wrap them in foil and put them in the oven for ten minutes on a medium to hot setting.

Most of the techniques described in this book have been created using colours that require heat-fixing. Screen- and block-printing inks, stencil crayons, fabric paints, silk paints, felt-tip pens and transfer paints are all fixed by heat, as are the water-based guttas.

After heat-fixing, the dyes are permanent and may be washed in lukewarm water or dry-cleaned.

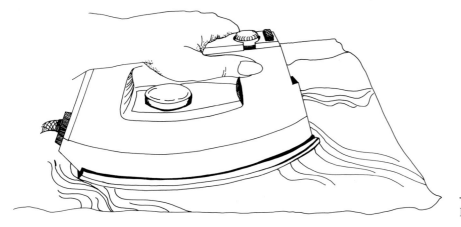

Fixing painted fabric with an iron

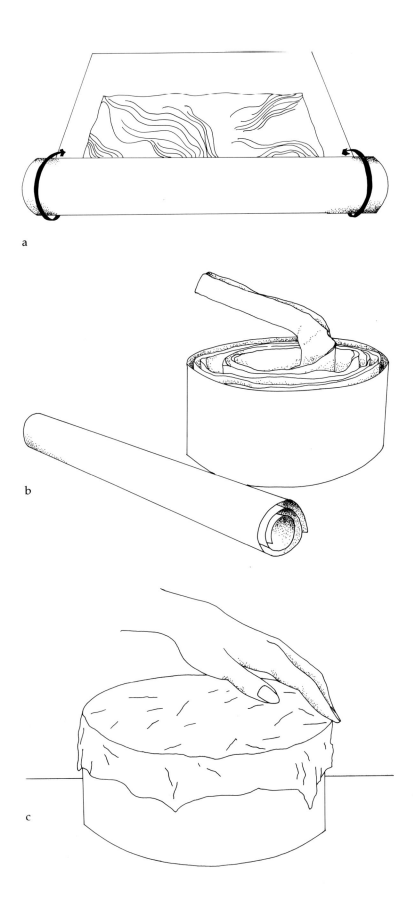

Steam-fixing

Silk-painting dyes will need to
be fixed in a steamer. There are
two types of commercially
available steamer, but it is also
possible to make your own
steamer using a pressure cooker.
Commercial steamers are
expensive and only viable if you
will be producing a lot of work.
Some large craft shops and
mail-order firms run a steaming
service, and your local dry-
cleaners may also have a steam
box.

Pressure cooker

The pressure cooker is useful for
smaller pieces of work. Place
each piece of fabric flat on top of
several layers of lining paper or

Preparing silk or wool for steam-fixing
in a pressure cooker.
(a) Roll fabric in absorbent paper
(b) Coil roll into container
(c) Cover container with tin foil
(d) Fabric steaming in pressure cooker

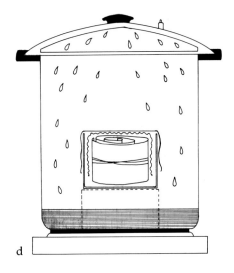

121

plain newsprint. Roll the fabric and paper together, then flatten and seal the ends with adhesive tape. Tuck the ends in towards the centre, then roll and flatten again to form a small, firm package.

Fill the bottom of the pressure cooker with water to a depth of about 2 cm (¾ in) and place in it a trivet. The water, even when boiling, must never reach the base of the trivet. To prevent the packages from becoming wet with the condensation from the lid, cover them with paper. Finally, cover the whole basket with a large sheet of foil so that the condensation runs down into the water. Seal the lid and steam for forty-five minutes.

Vertical steamer

The vertical steamer is a double-walled stainless-steel cylinder. The tube rests on a container of water. Some steamers are fitted with an element, but the manual steamer can be used in conjunction with a gas ring or electric hot-plate. The steamer is sealed at the top by a dome-shaped lid which has a hole in it. Steamers of this type can accommodate fabric up to one metre (39 in) wide, although an extension tube can be fitted for widths of up to 150 cm (60 in). Depending on the make of steamer, between thirty and fifty metres of fabric can be steamed at one time.

The fabric must be rolled in paper, and individual pieces of work must not touch each other.

Place the fabrics in the centre of the paper, leaving a margin of 5 cm (2 in) at each side. If metallic or black gutta, wax or sugar syrup have been used, another sheet of paper should be placed on top of the fabric for added protection. Roll the paper up and seal each end of the tube with foil and strong tape.

Lower the tube into the steamer, making sure that it does not touch the sides. Secure the top ring and seal with the dome-shaped lid. Fill the base container with water and then place the cylinder on top. Boil the water and steam for approximately three hours. Wool will need four hours.

Horizontal steamer

This is a long, stainless-steel box which can be heated on a cooker. It can accommodate approximately 18 metres (20 yards) of fabric up to 90 cm (36 in) in width. The water is held in the base of the box and steaming takes up to three hours.

If, when you remove your work from the steamer, you find watermarks or rings, it could be that you over-filled the base with water, or that there was inadequate protection. Gutta or sugar syrup sometimes sticks to the paper. Don't worry – it will come off when washed or dry-cleaned. If your fabric is badly creased, iron it before putting it into the steamer. If it is still creased, wash immediately in warm water and iron while damp.

Liquid-fixing

Some silk-painting dyes can be used in conjunction with silk-paint liquid fixer. Ensure that the fabric is dry and then coat or soak it in fixer to cure for approximately one hour. Rinse the fabric in warm water to remove the fixer and excess dye.

Dyebath dyes used in tie-dyeing and batik techniques can be fixed while being dyed. A cold-fix fixative is available to add to the dyebath, or some dyes need a solution to be made up to add to the dyebath. Check the manufacturer's instructions.

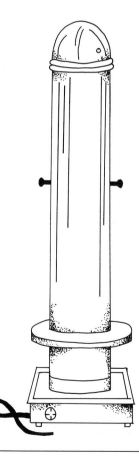

Vertical steamer

Air-curing

Dyes are available which do not need setting at all. They are set merely by leaving in the air for twenty-four hours. On some brands, a catalyst can be used to coat the fabric first; this helps the dyes to fix more quickly.

Dry-cleaning and washing

After fixing, your work can be washed or dry-cleaned. If you have used a resist such as wax or a solvent-based gutta, it is best to have it dry-cleaned, although these resists can be removed by an immersion in white spirit. The fabric must then be rinsed and washed several times to remove the smell. Do not soak the fabric, as some colours (especially red and black) have a tendency to run.

Even after commercial dry-cleaning, the fabric must be washed to remove excess dye. Dry-cleaning removes all the stiffness and returns the fabric to its original state. Do not dry-clean if you have used coloured or metallic guttas, or they will disappear.

After washing, lay the fabric on a clean towel, roll it up gently and pat to remove excess moisture. It is a good idea to iron the fabric straight away, while it is still damp, to remove any creases. If there is metallic or black gutta, puffa pens or outliners on the fabric, iron carefully on the back to prevent sticking.

Dipping fabric into a bowl of liquid fixer

EQUIPMENT AND PREPARATION

You will need to familiarize yourself with the equipment needed for each of the painting techniques. The specialist equipment required for specific techniques is explained in each chapter, but the following is a guide to the basic materials.

The workplace

All that is really necessary is a light, well-ventilated room, preferably with easy access to a tap and a power point. Be sure to cover all surfaces which could be spoiled by dyes with sheets of polythene and newspaper. Even those products which are fixed permanently by steaming and ironing later on will sometimes leave a mark on contact with furnishings. When using spray equipment, a fine mist of dye permeates the air and settles on all surfaces.

During the summer months you may prefer to work outdoors. Certain messy techniques such as tie-dye and spraying can easily be catered for outside, but beware of windy days with spraying techniques. The sun can also dry paints and dyes too quickly, preventing some of the additive techniques, such as salt and sugar, from working effectively. Your materials should be stored out of direct sunlight in a cool place. Do not allow them to freeze.

You could set up a special corner in a garage for very messy techniques such as flicking, spattering, squirting and spraying. Form a cardboard 'booth'; this will stop the paint from flying everywhere. Place newspaper on the floor to catch the drips.

Painting equipment

Tables

A large, firm, light-coloured table is ideal. If the space in which you will be working is required for other purposes, use a trestle table which can be packed away when not needed. Make sure that you can move easily around the table.

A fabric-printing table is slightly different. Fabric should never be printed on a hard surface. Cover a piece of chipboard with a thick blanket or piece of felt. Stretch and tack this smoothly over the surface, cover with a washable vinyl and tack firmly into place.

Frames

Many of the techniques require the fabric to be stretched taut above the worksurface. Art and craft shops stock a wide range of stretchers or frames made of wood and metal. A 'fixed' wooden frame is easily constructed using four pieces of soft wood cut to the required size. These can be glued or nailed together using butt or mitred joints.

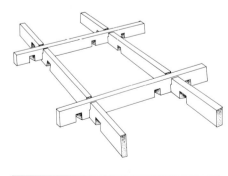

Adjustable 'slot' frame

More sophisticated frames can make finer adjustments, depending on the fabric size. The 'slot' frame and 'sliding' frame (which uses screws and wing-nuts) are much more versatile. A soft-wood adjustable 'slot' frame, which accommodates a 90 × 90 cm (36 × 36 in) piece of fabric, is most useful. Smaller pieces of fabric can be stretched across a tambour embroidery hoop or cardboard box.

Special frames for screen-printing can be bought from art suppliers. Marbling will also need a deep frame to 'pick up' large designs. Join together four pieces of wood, of the fabric length plus 5 cm (2 in), and 6 cm (2½ in) in depth. Place the frame on your worksurface and cover the base and insides with a thick sheet of polythene. Smaller solid trays could also be used to hold the liquid.

Pins

Use either push pins or specialist three-pronged architect's pins to secure fabric to the frame.

Preparing the fabric

Ensure that all fabrics are prepared for painting. Some fabrics contain dressing, or finish, added during manufacture, which should be removed by washing first in cold water and then in hot water with a mild soap. Some man-made fabrics require washing at low temperatures or should be dry-cleaned. If your fabric has a 'PFP' label, this indicates that the fabric is already 'prepared for painting'.

Always make sure that your dyes are absorbed into the fabric that you are using. Paint and then wash a sample to test the colourfastness. Do not use fabric softener in your water as this could inhibit the free flow of the dyes.

Stretching the fabric

Draw your design on to the fabric prior to pinning it on to a frame (see opposite). Pin on tightly, using the straight grain of the fabric as a guide. When dye is applied, the fibres often stretch, causing the fabric to sag, so re-stretch if necessary.

Brushes

Silk-painting brushes These wash brushes have a fine point but hold a large amount of dye at the base. They are recognizable by their wooden handles and wire-coil attachment of the hairs, and are available in many sizes. Rinse well after use. Never store with the points downwards, or in a sealed container.

Wax brushes Quality is not important with these brushes, as wax eventually destroys any brush. Flat-headed bristle brushes are ideal. A fine sable brush will be needed for delicate, intricate work, and a fan-shaped brush is most useful for creating textures. Brushes used with wax are impossible

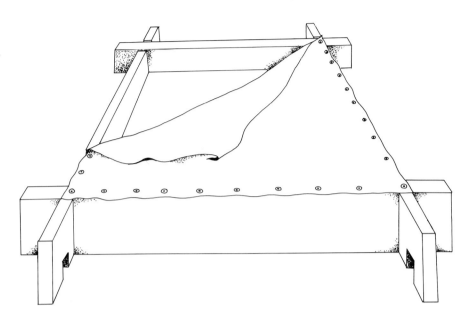

Fabric stretched and pinned on to a 'slot' frame

a ruler, a pair of compasses, white drawing paper, tracing paper, a kitchen roll, newspaper and masking tape may all be required.

Miscellaneous equipment

You will also need pots, jars, palettes, pipettes, a hairdryer, paper and fabric scissors, a Stanley knife, a cutting-board, a metal ruler, an iron and ironing-board, and dye-removing handcream or soap.

to clean, so they must be kept for this purpose only.

Stencil brushes These are inexpensive and readily available from art and craft shops in various sizes. They are short-handled with bristles forming a round shape. The flat tips enable you to dab the colour into the stencil shape.

Alternatives to brushes

Foam 'brushes' Available in many sizes, these are useful for painting large areas or thicker fabrics such as wool or calico.

Cotton wool, cotton pad and cotton bud Cotton wool or a cotton pad can be formed into a solid shape and clipped into a clothes' peg, making it ideal for painting large areas with even washes of colour. Cotton buds are useful for shading and texturing.

Sponges These are ideal for applying colour and texture, and for cleaning up the workplace. Natural sponges, although expensive, are worth the investment.

Drawing equipment

Magic marker pens, felt-tip pens, hard and soft pencils, a pencil sharpener, an eraser,

SAFETY IN YOUR WORKPLACE

- Provide adequate ventilation when spraying, and when using wax, alcohol and solvents.
- Wear a face-mask when mixing dye powders, chemicals and when spraying.
- Take care when using bleach or dyes for the flicking, spattering and splashing techniques.
- Check with your doctor if allergic reactions occur when using dyes or if you are pregnant. Use plastic gloves when possible.
- Solvents and alcohol are flammable; store them in airtight metal containers.
- Never heat wax in a dish on a naked flame. Invest in a thermostatically controlled wax pot.

MAIL ORDER AND STOCKISTS

BRITAIN

Fred Aldous
37 Lever Street
Manchester M60 1UX
(*Mail order and shop. Dylon, Pentel, Tulip and Pebeo, fabric-painting equipment and fabric crayons. Stencilling and marbling equipment and wax. Photograph image-maker*)

N.E.S. Arnold
Ludlow Hill Road
West Bridgeford
Nottingham NG2 6HD
(*Mail order. Batik, tie-dye and silk-painting equipment. Screen- and block-printing equipment. Fabrics, paints and dyes, transfer-printing inks, fabric crayons, pens*)

Edda Aschmann
Silk-painting Studio
Les Guilberts
Route de la Palloterie
St Peter's
Guernsey
Channel Islands
(*Fabric-painting equipment and books. Javana and Hobbidee*)

Atlantis Paper Co. Ltd
2 St Andrew's Way
London E3 3PA
(*Mail order. Sennelier silk dyes and fabric paints. Steamers, silk and equipment*)

Candle Makers Suppliers
28 Blythe Road
London W14 7DB
(*Mail order and shop. Deka, Knaijeff, Dylon, Pebeo, wax and steamers*)

Cornellissen & Son Ltd
105 Great Russell Street
London WC1B 3RY
(*Mail order and shop. Elbetex and Sennelier, silk dyes and fabric paints, steamers, wax, pearl-lustre pigments and bronze powders*)

Cowling & Wilcox
26–8 Broadwick Street
London W1V 1FG
(*Mail order and shop. Fabric-painting, airbrushing and lino-printing equipment. Marabu silk, Pentel, Setacolour*)

Dryad Specialist Crafts Ltd
P.O. Box 247
Leicester LE1 9QS
(*Mail order. Kits, fabric-painting and printing equipment. Courses available*)

Kemtex
Victoria Works
Wilton Street
Denton
Manchester M34 3RD
(*Mail order. Complete range of acid and reactive dyes for wool, silk and cotton. Fabric paints*)

Possi
North Barrow
Sparkford
Somerset BA22 7LW
(*Mail order. Javana, Marabu, fabric-painting equipment, silks, silk ties, ready-rolled scarves. Courses available*)

Procion Dyes
Noel Dyrenforth
11 Shepherds Hill
London N6 5QJ
(*Mail order. Procion cold-water-reactive dyes, tjantings, workshops*)

Rennies
61–3 Bold Street
Liverpool L1 4E2
(*Mail order and shop. Marabu, Dylon, Elbetex, Pentel, Deka. Airbrushing, screen-printing and marbling equipment. Stencils*)

Textile Techniques
5 Alexandria Street
Rawtenstall
Lancashire BB4 8HP
(*Mail order. Tjantings, tjaps, wax, batik cloth*)

The Painting on Silk Co.
22 Wainwright Road
Altrincham
Cheshire WA14 4BW
(*Mail order. Kits, dyes, silk, books and equipment. Hobbidee*)

Vycombe Ltd
High House
Parham
Woodbridge
Suffolk IP13 9CZ
(*Mail order. Pebeo, Deka, silk, ready-made scarves and ties*)

George Weil & Sons Ltd
The Warehouse
Reading Arch Road
Redhill
Surrey RH1 1HG
(*Mail order. Javana, Deka, Dupont, Speedball and Hunt, and Procion dyes. Everything you need for fabric painting. Screen-printing and marbling equipment*)

George Weil & Sons Ltd
18 Hanson Street
London W1P 7DP
(*Shop. Stock as above*)

EUROPE

Galerie Smend
Mainzer Strasse 31
Postfach 250360
5000 Cologne
Germany
(*Mail order, and superb shop and gallery with all your fabric-painting needs, including books and steamers*)

La Fourmi
Rue Vanderkinderen 236
1180 Brussels
Belgium
(*Shop. Dupont, Deka, Pebeo Ferfix fabrics, fabric-painting equipment, books, workshops*)

USA

Cerulean Blue Ltd
P.O. Box 21168
Seattle
Washington 98111
(*Mail order and shop. Procion dyes, cloud cover, Lumirie and Neopaque. Fabrics, equipment, cyanotype fabric and kits*)

Dharma Trading Co.
P.O. Box 150916
San Rafael
California 94915
(*Mail order and shop. Procion, Deka, Versatex, Sennelier, Pebeo, Jacquard dyes. Everything the fabric painter needs, including fabrics and steamers, cyanotype fabric and kits. Clothes made ready to paint, books, workshops*)

Ivy Imports
5410 Annapolis Road
Bladensburg
Maryland MO 20710
(*Mail order and shop. Vision Art (Aircure), Sennelier. Fabrics, equipment, workshops*)

AUSTRALIA

Canchem
P.O. Box 103
Avondale Heights
Victoria 3034
(*Mail order. Cyanotype chemical supplies*)

Detoro Pty Ltd
P.O. Box 324
Coogee
N.S.W. 2034
(*Mail order. Fabrics, dyes and painting equipment, books*)

FABRICS BY MAIL ORDER

BRITAIN

MacCulloch & Wallis Ltd
25–6 Dering Street
London W1R 0BH
(*All types of fabric*)

Pongees Ltd
184–6 Old Street
London EC1V 9PB
(*Silks*)

Pure Silk
Eddie Salter
Old Church Room
Hill Row
Haddenham
Cambridge CB6 3TL
(*Silk scarves*)

Robinson Hobbs
Jasmine Cottage
Ridge Lane
West Harptree
Bristol BS18 6ED
(*Silks*)

Whaleys (Bradford) Ltd
Harris Court
Bradford
West Yorkshire BO7 4EQ
(*All types of fabric*)

USA

Fabdec
3553 Old Post Road
San Angelo
Texas 76904
(*100% natural fibres: muslin, cotton, organdie, broadcloth, challis, crêpe. Dyes*)

Oriental Silk Co.
8377 Beverley Boulevard
Los Angeles
California CA 90048
(*Silks*)

Sureway Trading Enterprises
826 Pine Avenue
Suites 5 and 6 Niagara Falls
New York 14301
(*Good range of silks and wools*)

Test Fabrics
P.O. Box 420
Middlesex
New Jersey 06846
(*Silks and wools*)

Thai Silks
252 State Street
Los Altos
California 94022
(*Silks*)

INDEX